Millionaire Mindset: Steps

By Craig Beck

Copyright Viral Success Limited 2016

11th November 2016 – Seattle USA
For Jordan, go follow your dream.

The free companion downloads for these books are available at www.PowerfullyWealthy.com

Introduction

Shockingly almost 50% of people in the western world would be unable to raise $400 for a medical emergency without selling something or borrowing the money!

These same people believe that the system is stacked against them, their financial situation is not their fault and only the dishonest get rich. Let's be absolutely clear about this, wealth has nothing to do with working hard, luck, geography, ethics or genetics.

What you are about to discover in Millionaire Mindset is that money is just a made up concept; it doesn't really exist in the way that most people think that it does. When you wire someone some money, nothing physically moves. Currency is not loaded on to a van and delivered to the bank of your recipient! In reality, only a few numbers change on a computer screen somewhere.

Your dreams are also just an imagined concept but without the same social conditioning and rules that we apply to money. In your dreams you can fly, walk on water or be a superhero, all because nobody ever told you that you are not allowed to! This book will change the way you think about wealth and give you a step-by-step route to a rapid and continuous influx of money.

Millionaires are not all found in one zip code, one gender or one skin color. Abundance is available to anyone, from anywhere if they will only apply the correct mindset to allow money to flow into their lives.

Warning! I only offer this information to people who are prepared to do things differently. If you don't believe you can ever be a millionaire then don't buy this book. Because I can tell you now, you are right!

So You Want To Be Rich?

"Character cannot be developed in ease and quiet. Only through experience of trial and suffering can the soul be strengthened, ambition inspired, and success achieved",
Helen Keller

So you want to be rich?
Really?
How badly do you want it?

Think hard about this and say out loud a score out of one hundred. Lets say that zero is 'I have no desire at all to become a millionaire' and one hundred is 'I will do whatever it takes, I will work eighty hours a week, I will give up drinking with the boys/girls, I will give up taking vacations for the next five years, I will go without sex if you say that's what is required… I don't care what it takes I am doing it'.

Now think of your score!

If your score is under ninety-nine, you are in trouble. Maybe you shot straight out of the gate with a loud and proud one hundred because that's obviously the score I am looking for but most people are naturally a little reserved. They try to be positive but not crazy positive and so they say something like ninety percent or heck even ninety five percent.

Let's work with ninety five percent as an example. The fact that they bought this book says that they are pretty certain that they want to be wealthy, but maybe there is a something in their head pulling them back from the total commitment level that is really required. Perhaps they were told enough times that wanting money is bad or greedy. Or perhaps they have heard that only the corrupt people of the world are rich and it is more pure to live a normal everyday life. A lot of people get very spiritual about this and say that money is not important in the grand scheme of this wonderful life we have been gifted. Love, peace and happiness are all more important than money.

I can guarantee you that any person who ever said anything like that didn't have a lot of money, most of them were stone cold broke. These sorts of statements sound like they come from a higher, more moral place and can make us feel ashamed about craving wealth. Do not listen to these statements; they actually come from a very low and dark place. You see, even though a statement such as 'love is more important than money' sounds like an enlightened thing to say, it is making a dangerous assumption. It assumes that you can't have both at the same time. It's a bit like saying oxygen is more important than nitrogen when it comes to breathing. That may sound logical but the reality is we don't breathe pure oxygen and if we did we would die pretty quickly. The air we breathe is made up of 78.09% nitrogen, 20.95% oxygen, 0.93% argon, 0.04% carbon dioxide, and small amounts of other gases. If you only allowed yourself the oxygen then it would attack and kill your central nervous system and you would drop down dead.

The same is true of love, happiness, peace and any other fluffy ideal that you can come up with. I am not denying that love is important, vital in fact but it is not a universal solution to all your needs. You can't pay your credit card bill with love, if you get sick and go to hospital they won't accept a huge donation of happiness in return for your treatment. Let's be absolutely clear about some things, yes love is important but you can't compare it to money and say it's more important. That would be like saying the San Francisco Forty Niners are a much better football team than the San Francisco Giants. We are not comparing apples with apples; it is simply not a fair comparison.

Before you take another step on this journey you must get absolutely clear that money is not dirty or evil, it doesn't make you a bad person and it doesn't limit your ability to love or be loved. Money is freedom and that is all. Having an abundance of money means you are not trapped into a corner by life. If a family member gets sick you don't have to join the queue to see a cheap and inferior doctor. You have options open to you, and the more options you have in life the better and the richer you will be (and I am not just talking financially).

Nothing demonstrated the devastation of having restricted options quite like the horrific events of 9/11. Do you remember watching those shocking news reports of people jumping from the **twin towers**, knowing for certain that they were leaping to their deaths? In that stark situation they had two options and two options only. To burn to death or jump to their death, if they had had just one more option, anything, they would have taken it.

Once you have the mindset that gives you options you must choose one and live, breathe and eat it! The path you choose should consume you, not because I am telling you that it must but because no other state exists. If you have to force yourself to follow a certain prescribed path then you will never reach your full potential. Back when I was in my twenties a good friend of mine came to me with a business idea. He was so enthusiastic about it, I could feel the passion and energy radiating off him as he spoke. He was one hundred percent committed to the concept but he needed my help to get started. He wanted me to be a 50-50 partner on the venture. I won't go into a lot of detail but let me tell you that the project involved bulk importing socks and retailing them around the United Kingdom. I turned him down; actually I turned him down more than a dozen times in the end. I didn't feel the slightest bit of passion for what he was proposing. I knew I couldn't get excited about socks and I knew my purpose here in this life was not to warm the feet of my fellow man. I could have given it a go with my lukewarm mindset and done my best but I knew even back then that the most we could achieve would be something between mediocre success and abject failure.

This is why I am constantly telling people that if they are currently doing a job that they don't absolutely love then their first mission is to change that situation and as soon as possible. You will never get rich by pushing a bolder up a hill for someone else. If you don't jump out of bed in the morning and run into work, then you my friend are in the wrong line of work. Sadly most people realize this but get trapped in the loop of making ends meet and never have the courage to change the thing that is making them the most miserable.

Yes, you need desire by the bucket load if you are going to become a wealthy man or woman. You need to be working on your passion, a project that burns in your heart and soul like a raging inferno. There is a monumental difference between what you want in life and what you are driven to achieve. A burning desire is not the same as what you wish for. You might wish you will win the lottery but surely you can see that can't be the whole point of your life. A burning desire is not the same as what you want, you may aspire to owning a Bentley, but if you get it will it mean your life is complete? A burning desire is something that it is a MUST for you. You cannot live without it.

Just imagine, if you are in a desert now, it's so insanely hot and you have been exposed to the blazing sun for so long that you know you can only survive a little longer in these conditions, death is approaching fast. Suddenly you see a man on a camel approaching and he is holding a bottle of water. You straight away scramble to him and ask for water. Now, what if that person doesn't want to give you his water? Would you accept no for an answer, would you shrug and say 'oh ok, no problem'? Or would you do whatever it took to get some of his water?

Let me give you another example and make this absolutely clear for you. Assume that you don't know how to swim. While on vacation you go out for a walk in the middle of the night and you accidently fall into the deep end of the swimming pool. You wouldn't shrug and think 'it would be really nice to get out now'. You would kick and scream like your life depended on it. Getting out of that pool would be a burning desire, you would do anything in that moment to get the outcome in your mind.

Many people want to be a Millionaire, but most of them will never get anywhere near achieving it because it is not a must for them. If something is a must for you, you will do whatever it takes to get it. This is the burning desire that you need if you want to success in your life. Success never comes automatically; you will need to spend a lot of time and effort on it. If you are serious about committing all your effort to this goal in your life then carry on with this book. If you can't get yourself to one hundred percent committed then stop now, because you are just wasting both our time. Getting the Millionaire Mindset is a bit like pregnancy; you can't be half hearted about having a baby and decide to just get a little bit pregnant. The concepts behind PowerfullyWealthy.com are a binary proposition, you either want this or you don't. When I asked you at the start of this book to give me a score between zero and one hundred you may have believe there were one hundred and one possible answers, but what I am telling you now is there are only two. You can choose zero or one hundred and that is it!

I will close this chapter with a story from one of my all time favorite motivational speakers. Zig Ziglar is sadly no longer with us but I love the way he would tell stories to get across his point:

There was a wealthy oil man in Texas and he had a beautiful daughter. His daughter was of an age that he felt it was appropriate for suitors to bid for her hand in marriage. And the Oil Man was very protective of his daughter. He felt there really wasn't any one good enough to have her hand in marriage.

So he hosted very large party and invited the most eligible bachelors from all over. And during this party people mingled while having a good time and all the handsome men prepared to woo the oil man and his soon to be wealthy daughter. To these single guys it all seemed too good to be true, they were wondering what was the catch for this party. At the appropriate time the wealthy Oil Man brought everyone out to the pool. It was a very long pool. And the pool was full of Alligators.

All of the eligible bachelors were told to wait at one end of the pool and the Oil man with his daughter was at the other end. He proceeded to make an announcement:

"The first suitor willing and able to jump in the water and swim across this pool filled with alligators will have my daughter's hand in marriage. And not only would you be getting my daughter's hand in marriage but you will be getting first rights to all of this ... My estate and wealth".

No sooner had he finished his sentence than he heard a single big splash in the pool. He turned around quickly and was surprised to see a young man swimming as fast as he possibly could to get to the other end. Almost as fast as he had heard the splash, he was looking at this wet and out of breath young man standing in front of him. The oilman was surprised and shook the young man's hand. He then asked him what was his motivation for jumping into the pool full of alligators and swimming across? Was it his daughter's hand was it the wealth? Young man still out of breath responded, "Neither, I just want to know the who the of a gun is that pushed me in "

10th November 2016

"Success is getting what you want. Happiness is wanting what you get", Dale Carnegie

In the United States and the United Kingdom there is a huge sense of entitlement. The world has gone a little bit crazy, and it's mainly the fault of the media and marketing. We are constantly being sold the line that we deserve the best in life. Do you want a giant flat screen TV? Of course you do, and if you don't have the money don't let that stop you, just put it on a credit card and worry about it later. But the giant TV screen doesn't change the mindset of the person who bought it, they still think like a poor person but a poor person with a big television. After a while, when the majority have followed the 'you deserve it' line for long enough and they don't feel any better about their life they start to look for someone to direct their frustration at. Anyone will do, just so long as the finger of blame is kept firmly away from them. Brexit gave the people someone to blame.

They said 'It's not your fault that you are miserable and life is hard. The system has made you that way, the leaders before we came along were corrupt and unscrupulous'. Thus the fire of anger is ignited and because us humans will always take the path of least resistance, we are more willing to believe that someone else is to blame than we are to accept responsibility. The election of Donald Trump or the issuing of Article 50 by the United Kingdom will make absolutely no difference to the balance of wealth and abundance. In five years from now or twenty five years from now 80% of the population will be poor and 20% will be rich, exactly as it is today.

The reason this won't change the way most people hope and dream of a redress to the status quo is because the problem is not really where folk believe it to be. The cause of hardship and scarcity is not out there somewhere but rather inside the individual. So, the people who voted for change will sit and wait for someone else to do something, they will wait for someone to prove they were right all along. Meanwhile, the proportion of the 80% who wanted the UK to stay in Europe or for Clinton to continue the work of Obama will be certain that this is the end of the world as we know it and they will spend the next five years moaning and groaning, waiting for any opportunity to say 'I told you so, I knew I was right'. Both sets of people will remain in the 80%, but disillusioned and damn angry about it too.

Right here and now you have a decision to make, do you want to be right or do you want to be rich? Because you can't be both, right and wrong are just the subjective opinions of your ego and they have nothing to do with wealth, abundance, love and happiness. Giving events positive or negative labels is the action of the 80% and is the quickest route to scarcity.

It reminds me of an old story… Many years ago a wise peasant lived in China. He had a son who was the gleam in his eyes and a white stallion, which was his favorite belonging. One day his horse escaped from his grounds and disappeared into the fields outside the village. The villagers came to him one by one and announced their condolences. They said, "You are such an unlucky man. It is so bad." The peasant answered, "Who knows. Maybe it's bad, maybe it's good." The populous left, happy that such an unfortunately thing hadn't happened to them instead.

The next day the stallion returned followed by twelve wild horses. The same people returned and told our wise man about how lucky he was. "It's so good, you must be so happy." He replied once more, "Who knows. Maybe it's good, maybe it's bad."

As it happens, the next day his one and only son was attempting to break in one of the wild horses when the horse fell down and broke his son's leg in the process. Once more everyone came to console him. They said, "You poor man, it's so bad." Again he replied, "Who knows. Maybe it's bad, maybe it's good."

Three days passed and his unfortunate son was limping around the village with his broken leg, when the emperor's army entered the village announcing that a war was starting and they conscripted all the young men of the village. However, they left the son since he had a broken leg. Once more, everyone was so jealous of our man. They surrounded him talking about his shier luck. "It is so good for you," they said. He answered all thus, "Who knows. Maybe it's good, maybe it's bad."

The Millionaire Mind

"There are people who make things happen, there are people who watch things happen, and there are people who wonder what happened. To be successful, you need to be a person who makes things happen", Jim Lovell

Are you growing a little weary of watching other people fall on their feet and pick up what appears to be more than their fair share of life's riches? Perhaps you are so far away from what you think would be fair that you are currently struggling with debt and can't see a time when it will ever get any better.

Does it make you a bad person to want to escape the daily grind and struggle; is money really the route of all evil? The answer as you would expect from a book like this is a categorical no. The undeniable fact is money and wealth are just an idea, a creation of someone's imagination or perhaps a better label would be that of 'an illusion'. You see money as we believe it to be doesn't really exist. The dollar bills we see in our wallets are merely expensively printed IOU notes that promise we will pay our debt upon presentation of said bill. The debt never gets paid because money doesn't really exist. This becomes even more apparent when you deposit your cash into the bank and rather than store your personal currency in a special cupboard with your name on it (after all it's your money right?) your cash suddenly becomes physically invisible and changes to a series of numbers on a computer display.

You may be frowning at the book at this point and raising a fist to me while shouting 'it doesn't matter whether money is real or not Craig, I don't have as much as I want and that's why I bought your book'. Don't worry there is a good reason I am painstakingly going to lengths to make a factual if apparently pointless observation. Ideas are obviously just creations of the human mind and if we can agree early on in this book that money, wealth and therefore abundance are purely a creation of the mind then our journey to understanding why some people are drowning in the stuff and others are conversely up to their neck in debt becomes a whole lot simpler.

Let's be clear about something quite important, PowerfullyWealthy.com does not just teach people how to become rich. Being wealthy does not guarantee happiness and peace; if your only goal is to become rich then you are missing the point of the process. Money gives you freedom – the freedom to do more, help more and give more. But if you believe that money will bring you happiness in and of itself then I am afraid you are in for a disappointing lesson in life. Money is not happiness, it is the merely the byproduct of achieving happiness. Over the course of this book we are going to discover how to manifest the life of your dreams, to find your true purpose in life and fill that hole inside you that has always been there.

If you currently don't have as much wealth as you really want or desire then I want you to see this as a simple sign that the hole inside you is still there. Desiring more money is a symptom of a bigger problem but just as you can't cure the common cold by wishing you didn't have it. You can't get more money trying to wish it into your life. Wishing is always an expression of scarcity and despite what your parents told you when inviting you to blow out the candles on your birthday cake, wishes are never granted when they come from a point of scarcity.

Money, wealth and attainment are not the point of this book but we start with money for two reasons. Firstly because the vast majority of people start this journey assuming that if they had more money they would be happier. Because that hole inside you feels like it needs to be filled with something, money and material 'stuff' seem like the perfect fit. Let's be clear, there is absolutely nothing wrong with wanting more money and by taking this course you will be able to dramatically increase the amount you have and quicker than you ever expected to be possible. The really amazing news is that as exciting as that prospect may sound I want to tell you the other benefits are going to make all this extra wealth and abundance pale into insignificance. You are about to discover something profoundly beautiful and life changing. I am deeply excited to be here at the start of the journey with you.

Before we go any further, let's deal with some of the stigma attached to having and wanting money. Your elders, parents and religious teachers would have you believe that money is the work of the devil and only truly selfish and shallow people go off in search of it. Money is referred to as cold hard cash, which is 'nonsense'. Money isn't cold or hard, it's soft and warm and I don't believe for a minute that if I made my bed out of it I wouldn't have the best night's sleep of my life.

So why do some people have more trappings of success than other (often more deserving) people? To give you a really simple answer… we are all given two books of magic spells. One book creates pain, misery and lack. Meanwhile, the spells in the second book manifest love, wealth, abundance and happiness. Unfortunately neither book is labeled and the spells are written in a language that we don't understand.

The longer (and clearly necessary) answer is this. The world is a duality, everything is in perfect balance. Eastern religions explain it as 'yin and yang'. You can't choose to only have 'yin' in your life, you must also take the opposing 'yang' that comes with it. We often bemoan the unfairness of life and some people eventually use the struggle of life as proof that there cannot possibly be a loving God or divine creator. For if there were such a being he would surely not sit by and allow the suffering to continue. What we fail to see is that the things we want and desire in life could not exist without their counter position to give them context. As the saying goes *'even when you light a candle you cast a shadow'*. If everyone on planet earth had more money than they knew what to do with, would anyone give the slightest hoot as to how much something cost or whether their neighbor had a better car than them? Of course not, people want money because they have experienced (all too often) how it feels to have the opposite of abundance in this area. It is the very thing we hate that gives power and meaning to the thing we love.

Why do our loved ones die, sometimes painfully of horrendous diseases such as cancer and strokes? Again because without the concept of ill-health there is no context to being of good health. Try and think of one element of our existence that doesn't obey the laws of 'yin and yang', I know that you will fail this challenge. Everything is rotating in a circle, even the planet we stand on. There is no death without first there being life, there is no love with out having a polar opposite emotion to compare it to and there can be no happiness without the yang of sadness to give life to the state we desire.

Why do bad things happen to people? Because good things happen to people!

"If a man is crossing a river and an empty boat collides with his own skiff, even though he may be a bad-tempered man he will not become very angry. But if he sees a man in the boat, he will shout at him to steer clear. If the shout is not heard, he will shout again, and yet again, and begin cursing. And all because there is somebody in the boat. Yet if the boat were empty, he would not be shouting, and not angry. If you can empty your own boat crossing the river of the world, no one will oppose you, no one will seek to harm you…. Who can free himself from achievement, and from fame, descend

and be lost amid the masses of men? He will flow like Tao, unseen, he will go about like Life itself with no name and no home. Simple is he, without distinction. To all appearances he is a fool. His steps leave no trace. He has no power. He achieves nothing, has no reputation. Since he judges no one, no one judges him. Such is the perfect man: His boat is empty." — Osho

Within you there is a source of manifestation power that is capable of creating an abundance of anything you desire. This amazing and divine ray gun will amplify and magnify whatever you point it at. But here's the catch, there is no instruction manual and no safety switch. It doesn't warn you before you fire it and if you choose to point it at poverty that is exactly what you will get more of. So, you might think 'why don't people just make sure they point it at good things'? It's a good observation but it's not quite as simple as it appears. Noticing that your neighbor has a better car than you and deciding you want a better car as a result of this does not point the gun at manifesting an automobile. Instead the gun gets pointed at your jealousy and scarcity mindset. Rather than pulling up on your own drive a few days later in your new Mercedes you get more and more infuriated as you watch your neighbor get a pool installed and head off on his third vacation of the year.

The main reason we cast the wrong spells and point the magic ray gun at the opposite of what we want is we give control of the device to the voice that shouts the loudest. Do you remember being a small child at school when the teacher asked a question and you realized you actually knew the answer? Do you remember how high in the air you shoved your hand? So high that you had to use your other hand to support it and keep it defying gravity up there! Inside us there are two elements that direct the flow of our life. The soul (or subconscious if you would rather stay clear of any religious undertones) and the conscious or ego.

Humanity has a problem and quite a significant one; we perceive the ego to be a gift when in reality it is a curse. We believe the ego to be a unique facet of our individuality that gives us independence and character. The ego in reality is a fragment of our being that is quite frankly insane. Such is the insanity that it has even managed to convince us that bad is good and vice versa.

When we talk about the ego most people assume we are referring to one specific type of selfish behavior. However, the ego is so much more that that narrow band of negative patterns and yet that doesn't mean there is a good side to it, no aspect of the ego can be viewed in any sort of positive light or considered an advantage to the human existence.

The ego really is the insane part of our physiological make up and absolutely nobody is free of it, not even the most enlightened being. We all have differing strengths of ego and ergo according levels of insanity that present themselves in a myriad of different ways that we might label as character traits or personality.

The first thing you should know of this part of you, is that the ego cannot ever be satisfied, it can only ever be sedated temporarily. Like a naughty child at the 'all you can eat' ice cream factory it will always want more no matter how much it gets, even if more of what you crave is in the long run detrimental to your well being. It is for this reason alone that giving a person the exact amount of money they have declared will bring peace is only effective as a temporary sticking plaster solution to their problems. Very soon reasons why that amount was too conservative begin to emerge.

Unhappiness, pain and misery are human emotions created directly by the ego to manipulate a desired response. These painful feelings are generated by the 'thinking mind' when it doesn't get what it wants but also rather ironically also directly as the result of giving it exactly what it wants too, such is the insanity!

Think of the soul/subconscious as silent but powerful and the ego as noisy but weak. Because the ego has his hand in the air and is screaming for our attention we get mixed up about which part of us is weak and which part is powerful. It is natural to assume the element of our being that is jumping up and down and assuring us that it knows what to do is the best holder of the ray gun. This is wrong, wrong, wrong – we inadvertently give the keys to the asylum to the most dangerous inmate.

The ego insists it knows how to use the ray gun to give you what you want. Like a baby who has just had its lolly pop taken from him, it will scream blue murder until you give it what it wants. But, your ego can achieve peace only for the tiniest fragment of time, normally immediately after you give it what it wants. For the briefest of moments it affords you a small break from the insanity and stops relentlessly punishing and manipulating you. When the sedation begins to fade the ego reawakens as ravenous as a grizzly bear stirring from a long hibernation. It demands more of what you gave it before but ten times stronger and will not accept anything but your capitulation, sending massive pain in the form of a hundred different negative emotions such as jealousy, low self esteem and self loathing until it gets what it desires. This is the exact reason why 95% of diets fail, trying to arm wrestle the egoic mind into submission with a technique incorrectly labeled as 'will power' is like trying to move a mountain with a spoon.

Nobody has ever achieved anything with 'will power' because it's an oxymoron there is actually no power involved in it at all! The ego cannot be strong-armed into submission by defiance; it has you outgunned on every level. Your ego has the power to cause you pain beyond your wildest nightmares and it isn't afraid to use it. The only way you achieve anything of significance in life and beat the discontentment of the ego is by harnessing the divine power of the subconscious. At this level of being you are capable of limitless joy, anything and everything is possible without the need for anything to make it possible. From mild contentment to perfect peace and everything in between your subconscious mind has the power to deliver it to you. This is what I call 'The Millionaire Mindset'; it is the other book of spells that you have rarely used. This book is in such pristine condition because you unwittingly asked the (insane) ego which book was best to use in order to get the life you want.

Until this point I have carefully used the word subconscious when really I would have preferred to say soul. I do this deliberately because for me to expect you to accept the word soul (and all its connotations) I have to make an assumption that you believe it exists in the first place. Virtually everyone accepts the concept of a conscious and a subconscious, I can comfortably bring these aspects of the human mind up nice and early in the book but I wait until this point hoping to have whet your appetite before I appear to go 'all spiritual' on you!

For me your soul and your subconscious are one and the same because what happens to you unconsciously and by that I mean without the interference of your ego or your thinking mind, happens with divine power. By divine I mean there is simply nothing that is impossible if your soul or subconscious so desires it. Naturally, the first skeptical objection to this grand claim of miracles is challenging statements like 'if I am all powerful, why aren't I rich already' and so on.

The deeper answer to that question you will discover as you journey through this book, but as a tempting morsel to keep you going; and of course to avoid 'question dodging' accusations flaring up so early in our relationship as author and reader I would ask you to consider that it is only your ego that believes you need money to be happy. Anything that has it's solution in the future is pure speculation of your conscious mind, one of those specific requirements of how happiness should be packaged for your consumption. Your soul doesn't believe anything; it desires nothing, needs nothing and it automatically knows what will make you happy.

As a natural born cynic myself, I will try and answer your logical objections as we discover these secrets together. By this point I understand that your mind is probably acting like the Hydra beast of Greek mythology; for every question I answer two new ones appear to take its place. This is the ego again attempting to reassert its authority and we have been taught from an early age to listen to it.

From childhood we are told that to want too much is to be greedy, rich people are immoral and somehow tainted by their own success. Conversely to not have enough money, to be poor is also judged to be a failure. We project this confusing concept out to the masses through our movies, books, television news and tabloid newspapers. We love the underdog until they become successful and then we demand that they are brought down a peg or two.

Society wants us to have 'just enough' but not quite enough to be happy – this is what we have collectively agreed is 'normal' which for some reason when you write it down appears to be quite insanely ridiculous. Our parents also subscribed to this standpoint, as did their parents and all who went before them. It's the bizarre relay race of the ego forever passing its delusions onto the next generation. This is demonstrated by our parents in the vocalized desire for us to work hard and get a 'good job' to ensure our future happiness. What parents mean by a 'good job' is a safe and secure job that may even be boring but is continuous. Rarely do parents hope and dream that their children will follow their heart, throw caution to the wind and take risky, dangerous but exciting jobs.

There are many millions of people around the world in the most menial and insignificant of low paid, unskilled jobs that are content with their lot and truly happy within themselves, but no parent would wish or encourage this lifestyle for their child. Instead their aspirations for their young are generated from the ego and they dream that they will be the world's next doctors, scientists, accountants, managers and directors. Hopefully, along the way they will meet the man or woman of their dreams, settle down with a mortgage (a word derived from the Latin phrase meaning until death) have kids and live happily ever after, only to repeat the process again.

A list of handed down expectations that compound the belief that happiness is a destination achievable through the attainment or attachment to external things. They want this for us because it's what they want for themselves and therefore assume it is also the best that could happen to us. This belief is an oasis in the desert to the thirsty man, nothing but a pure illusion.

This cycle has been running in the western world for many thousands of years but recently levels of general unhappiness and frustration have begun to accelerate and magnify exponentially as a result of the stabilizing prop of traditional religion beginning to fail simultaneously. The discontented folk could previously be dissuaded from challenging the status quo with assurances that God has a place in heaven reserved for them, but only if they comply with the rules and dare not question the scriptures further.

In order to achieve abundance we have to consider the reverse of that position, as a result of this premise of human programming you will find that this book is not an instruction manual or a journey of discovery. If anything it's about the opposite of learning, an unlearning experience where we slowly strip away the false beliefs that you have been programmed and burdened with since birth.

When a fishing trawler gets trapped in a violent storm what brings the respite is the removal of something and not the addition of something. The removal of the storm and a return to zero is what dissipates the sensation of peril and danger. As such, happiness is peace and peace is the absence of everything else and so it's illogical to assume we can find what we are looking for by creating rules or by attaining material possessions. Abundance comes as the direct by product of happiness and is not the destination we are navigating to.

The secrets revealed in this course will change your life forever and your discovery of it at this point in your life is no coincidence. As the famous quotation goes; 'when the student is ready, the teacher will arrive' and for that reason, despite your excitement you cannot force this information onto others who do not seek it, do not expect them to receive the message with the same sense of wonder and excitement that you did.

Most people spend their entire lives trapped within the illusions of the egoic mind. However, a small and rapidly increasing number of people are awakening during their lifetime to realize the futility of their beliefs about what they think they 'need' to discover true wealth and abundance on earth. You are one of the enlightened few that are ready to discover that the universe always ignores the dreams of your ego. However, using the core principles described in this book you will soon be able to manifest your dreams quickly and easily using the power of your subconscious and your connection to the manifestation magic that resides within you.

Research shows us that of all the things you hear in a 24-hour period, 80 percent of them are negative. The average 18-year-old male has been told 146,000 times no or you can't do it. Now this causes us a problem because of something I call the law of subconscious attraction (or subattraction for short). Basically you have delivered to you what you subconsciously know to be true. If you simply know, and I do mean absolutely 'know' that you are an overweight individual then that reality will be created for you whether it's currently true or not. If at a subconscious level you fundamentally believe life is meant to be spent struggling to pay the bills and living hand to mouth (Perhaps just like your parents did) then guess what happens.

The egoic world in which we live would have you believe a whole heap of negative bullshit, because misery loves nothing better than company. In short eighty percent of the world is throwing a pity party and has extended you a big fat invitation. At the moment you are still on the guest list and what I am suggesting to you; is that if you change your beliefs not only can you leave the others to their depressing party but you can join the world's elite twenty percent who want for nothing and live the life of their dreams.

Now of course I am not suggesting that cash automatically brings happiness, but then the PowerfullyWealthy.com course is not really about wealth, it's actually about success. Wealth is purely the byproduct of that achievement and nothing more. To be successful and happy you must be a success on three levels. Spiritually, with your health and with your finances. If you are rich but your health is poor you are not a success. If you are spiritually connected and you are healthy, but you are poor, you are not a success. Get one area wrong and your life is completely different. These three essential elements must remain intact like the spokes of a bicycle wheel or the integrity of the whole structure collapses.

A frequently made mistake is looking at someone who is rich and assuming that they are therefore happy. The people who are the most content in life never set out to become wealthy, they just did what made them happy, what they were passionate about and the money just flowed in as an automatic outcome of their harmony with the universe. On the flip side there are many thousands of wealthy individuals who focused purely on the outcome rather than the journey. We all know that we could become fabulously wealthy in minutes if we would just pick up a sawn off shotgun and wander with some menace down to the nearest savings bank. For most of us we can already see that even if we did get away with the crime we still wouldn't be happy with our new situation.

So what is the foundation for financial abundance? Having enough money to live on and then some. More money than you really need. It's a very empowering feeling. Imagine thinking you can do absolutely anything you want. You really can be the best that you can be because you can buy any material, any service. You can go anywhere and any when. That is what we are talking about with The Millionaire Mindset. The ability to be the very best that you can be. To have the very best that life can offer, the best healthcare, the best car and the best house. Everything designed to make sure you can live your life to the best.

Like everything solid you must build success on strong and lasting foundations. Life is about a chain of moments and your success depends on the choices you make in your daily actions. It's not about what you do as a one-off, it's not about that grand gesture that you just do one day. If you want to get fit you don't just go for a jog one day and then decide that you're fit, you do it every day. It's those actions in life that become habits that really change your life and move you forward.

I'm going to suggest to you many changes this book. Even if you don't believe in them or you doubt whether they will work, I would like to ask a favor of you. I would like to ask you to do them for just 21 days every day.

If after 21 days you decide they are not working for you, then that's fine. But I know they will work for you because after 21 days they pass from the thinking mind into the divine subconscious and become a habit. This new physical pathway allows you start to do them every day without having to make a conscious decision to do so. Before no time, they start to make a massive positive impact on your life. You'll see yourself turning towards wealth. You'll see your bank balance increase and you'll see your commitment to achieve that wealth grow day by day.

Happiness, peace and purpose are not things that are stumbled upon by the lucky few. All these states are the by-product of running a specific program in life. Yes, there is a recipe to success and if you follow it to the letter you can't help but achieve the desired outcome. There are FIVE ingredients to long-term growth and change and they are:

Desire; - and I'm guessing you probably have quite a lot of that. People who are not driven to succeed do not buy books like this one. I can't emphasize this enough; the fact that you are listening to this material speaks volumes about you and your intent. Truly eighty percent of the people you meet will never in their lifetime spare the time or the money to invest in a book like this. It's probably quite logical then that we know that twenty percent of the population own eighty percent of the wealth in the world.

Knowledge; before the captain of an ocean liner changes course he first must know in which direction the ship needs to go. Gaining the information you need is a fundamental step in the process of developing a millionaire mindset. Good news, investing in self-improvement audiobooks like this one is a clear indication how firmly on the path you are.

Skill; when you learn something new. Initially it resides in your conscious mind and requires active thought to complete the task. For example, when you learn to speak a new language, initially it's difficult and you have to think carefully about each and every word before you say it. Eventually over time you gain confidence and the process passes to the subconscious mind, at this point you have a skill and the once difficult challenge becomes an automatic process.

Action; doing what has to be done. That is so important because people put off things that are so important that they can't be put off. It can't wait until tomorrow. Your wealth must start now, this instance. If you stop the CD [transcription from the audiobook] and don't do something towards your wealth, you're wasting your time. You must take action and do it.

Applying these four simple principles to your life pushes you firmly into the top twenty percent of the western population. So many people go through life in a boring job they hate, nine-to-five, saying to themselves daily 'I don't like this job, I hate my boss and I can't wait for the weekend… but you know I play the lottery and maybe one day I'll win the big jackpot and then I can get started on living the life I want'.

Do you know how many of those people do go on to win the big jackpot? It's not many. For most forty nine ball lottery draws your chance of scooping the jackpot is over 14,000,000 to 1. In real terms you have much more chance of being eaten by a shark than you have of winning your fortune in this game of chance.

Interestingly In Ireland, there was a survey among people a few years ago asking them about their greatest wish. More than anything else - much much more, people wanted to ... win the lottery.

And it is interesting to consider whether winning the lottery makes people happy. Research shows that the answer is a very restricted ... yes. It makes them happy for a short time. However, studies have shown that people get much more satisfaction by earning their money than winning it. In addition, the boost in happiness from a lottery win has been shown to dissipate over time. Studies of past lottery winners shows that happiness levels typically return to where they were prior to the big winning. Even more surprising, one man who won $315 million in a lottery reported significant unhappiness and feeling of being "cursed".

When you are looking outside for solutions you will have to accept the negative that comes with the positive.

I have the good fortune to work in the media industry and I spend a lot of time coaching broadcasters and journalists helping them craft their on air style to appeal to as broad an audience as possible. Radio and television is a numbers game and these guys get paid on their ability to make real, everyday folk like them. The problem a lot of broadcasters face is one of lack of real world experience, they have always been in media, which lets be honest is a cushy little number. Most of them have never done a hard days work in their lives. They have never worked a real job and are faced with the daunting prospect of trying to be relatable to the very people who they have no experience of communicating with on a daily basis.

I sometimes tell them a story about my friend Mike, who works in a meat processing plant. Mike hates his job, beyond his friends who work there with him there is absolutely nothing he likes about his daily grind (for that is exactly what it is, a grind). People who love their jobs like the weekends but they don't see them as the only worthy part of a seven day week. Mike starts planning his weekend on a Tuesday, everyday in the break room he talks about what he plans to do on Friday and Saturday night. Then when the weekend comes around he finally feels alive, on a Sunday he tells me he stays up as late as he can because he knows as soon as he goes to sleep his weekend is over and another tedious week begins.

Don't underestimate how many people spend an entire lifetime trapped in this depressing routine, many never considering that there may be a way out of the loop. These are the eighty percent of the population who represent the bums on seats commercial radio and television stations see as their meat and drink.

It's this mass acceptance of a life full of scarcity that keeps generations trapped in poverty. Recent research has shown us that if you take 100 men aged 25, follow them through life and meet them again at age 65, do you know, out of those that have survived, how many are wealthy?

Five. Just five. That means up to 95 others are so poor that they're living on the state for the vast majority of their lives, and why is this the case? Simply because they accept the prescribed reality that life is a struggle but for a lucky few who one day might be lifted out of the despair by six multicolored balls dropping in the correct sequence.

These sorry individuals are responding to life as it happens to them rather than creating their own universe. This is like being given the winning lottery numbers but refusing to buy the ticket. You have the inbuilt divine power to manifest your own reality but you have to do something now. If you want to be wealthy take action, Today is the day.

The fifth ingredient to long-term growth and change is persistence. In other words, creating habits and not will power based goals. It's not what you do as a one-off, it's what you do every day that will grow wealth and abundance for you.

All five of these characteristics are necessary for long-term growth. If any one is lacking, long-term change will not occur at all. Many people try to take shortcuts around one or more of them, and the biggest problem is most people try to go straight from desire to action without pausing to acquire the necessary knowledge or skills.

In other words, people want more money and try and go and get it, but they don't really know how they're going to get it. Thankfully it's a little bit different for you because you've acknowledged that you need to do that and you've bought this audiobook. I'm guessing that this won't be the only MP3 or book that you buy on the subject. That's good. Keep going. The more knowledge you have, the more you have to use.

Some people do a little bit better. They'll go through the first three steps; desire, knowledge and skill but then they just can't get themselves to act. Or they accomplish the first four steps and then they get stumped when change doesn't happen all at once and they give up. They fail to be persistent. They fail to turn their new, good deeds, into habits. They're just one-offs. They get a little bit of progress and then nothing and they give up.

So remember, if the principles, questions and skills I offer you, are to result in long-term sustainable growth they must become habits. Nothing short of a habit will work for the long haul.

I am sure you have already read about 'The Law of Attraction', Rhonda Byrne's 'The Secret' and countless self-help gurus who advocate that the secret to manifesting the life of your dreams is hidden somewhere in their positive thinking mantra. Or perhaps after you have recited your positive affirmations enough times, only then you will finally get what you are looking for. I am willing to go out on a limb here and take a guess that you have tried all that 'stuff' and found it at best inconsistently successful. Maybe you got a little success but certainly nowhere near the life you dream of!

Of course, this is an easy prediction to make, because why would you be reading this book if the other stuff had worked the way you had hoped?

Why are some people poor and other people rich? Why are some people happy with a little bit of money and others miserable with millions of dollars? What makes one person popular and their company sought after and another despicable and avoided at all cost? What is the truth behind positive thinking and how can it help you?

The fact is that the conventional understanding of positive thinking and its techniques is misunderstood and misused by millions of people. It often produces the opposite of what you want in the first place.

I get annoyed sometimes when I hear people bleating on about positive thinking and how it can get you anything. You can get anything and you can do anything you want if you just think positively about it. It's absolute rubbish. I don't care how positively I think about it, I could not be a professional football player. I could not join the English Premier League and expect to keep up or perform on the same level as the other footballers. I don't care how positive and how many great things I say to myself, I know that I couldn't go up to an explosive device and defuse it and even dream of staying in one piece.

One of the best motivational speakers America ever produced, Zig Ziglar, summed this up perfectly when he said "positive thinking will not let you do anything but it will let you do everything better than negative thinking".

If you're currently doing a job that you cannot be positive about, you just cannot bring yourself to think anything positive about it, get out of that job now. You will never become wealthy or rich in that job.

Did you know that 80 per cent of the world's workforce hates their job? In fact hate probably isn't a strong enough word, they DESPISE their job. They turn up, they put their head down and for eight hours they hate, hate, hate their job.

Negative, negative, negative flows through every fibre in their body. That means that people on average everywhere are spending about 40 hours every week doing something they hate and trying to get wealthy doing it. It's stupid, it will not work. It's time to wake up and smell the coffee... You can only be successful in life if you're doing what you enjoy.

Why's that so? Well it's because you're performing the work of your heart and soul, what you enjoy. You create a special vibration with your thoughts and your emotions. Your thoughts become positive automatically, you don't have to work at it. You're always a positive thinker when you're doing something you enjoy.

If you are currently doing a job you don't enjoy, that you're doing merely to pay the bills and keep the wolves from the door, you will not become rich. It's not the way to success. Your job or life's work should not be something you hate, especially when it takes up most of your energy, your creativity and your life.

It's my deepest desire that with the help of this audiobook you will discover for the first time in your life what you really, honestly, truly want. That coupled with the practical application of the skills in this series of books to transform you into a shining beacon of happiness, peace and purpose.

Of course I don't know you personally, and the chances are good that we have never met. However, I believe that even without meeting you I already know two fundamental things about who you are, how you feel and what you really want to happen next. If you are anything like me, you will have always had a nagging sensation that you are here to do something important. You understand there is great potential inside you and life has an important mission for you. This sensation is what Nazi war camp survivor Victor Frankl described as the existential vacuum. It is literally a black hole in your being that is created by the failure to follow your heart and complete the task that you are really here to do. This hole is painful and uncomfortable, it is always there at the background of your existence and it won't go away until you fill it back up.

My brother in law once set up a business called SAHAFI. I asked him what the company does and he replied 'anything'. Being rather confused by his answer I asked what the name meant and he revealed that it was an acronym for 'See A Hole And Fill It'. This is an instinctive response of human beings and we approach this internal vacuum with the same sticking plaster approach. We know there is a dull ache inside us created by this emptiness and so we desperately try to fill it up. Our favorite ways to do this are with material possessions, sex, drugs and alcohol and all other things earthly and physical. This universally pursued attempt to fill the hole is as effective as trying to fill a volcano by throwing matchsticks into it. Fruitless, pointless and a waste of time!

How many people do you know who give everything they have to climb the corporate ladder, to get onto the next pay scale to get the car with upgraded leather interiors?

How many people do you know choose where they live or the car they drive by comparing it to what their friends and neighbors have?

How many people do you know who max out their credit card so they can have a television at least two inches bigger than their friends have?

Does it ever make any of them happy, I mean truly a genuine sensation of peace and contentment with life? Maybe for a few days, even possibly for a few weeks but never (and I really do mean never) for a lifetime. Money, cars, boats, houses, vacations, gadgets, technology and all this other 'stuff' we dream of owning are nothing more than matchsticks for the volcano. I don't know what your true purpose in life is but I do know that it is not to own a great automobile or only ever stay in five star hotels. Over this series of books you are going to discover what you need to fill that vacuum inside you. When the hole is filled you are going to find that love, peace, happiness and joy floods into your life. All the things that you thought would bring happiness, such as money, sex, vacations and abundance are not actually how you create happiness they are the result of being happy. The whole of the western world has got the whole puzzle the wrong way around. When you fill the vacuum then all the good stuff will automatically flow into your life.

I am deadly serious about this, there is no limit to the amount of money, abundance and love that can flow into your life just as soon as you start to travel in the direction you were always meant to follow. Let me ask you a question.

What do you want more than anything right now?

Whether that answer is physical or emotional, let me tell you that you can have it. But, only when you stop trying to force life to give it to you. Perhaps you want to meet the man or woman of your dreams. Maybe you have started to think that you will be on your own forever. Or are you one of those serial monogamists that go from one short and often dramatic relationship to the next, without ever finding that special person who you want to share the rest of your life with. Or perhaps you are the guy that never seems to get the break at work, missing out on promotions that you know you are more than capable of rising to?

Don't worry all these situations are just symptoms of the black hole inside you, pulling the exact opposite of what you want towards you. Once we fill this hole, the gravity of life will change. Literally, just like flipping a magnet the opposite way around, suddenly what was once pulled into your path will now be repelled. And all the good stuff such as the money, love, amazing relationships, success and peace will become drawn towards you.

Human nature causes us a little problem at times, we tend to be increasingly impatient and want the magic bullet cure for everything right now! We also tend to lean toward the incorrect assumption that happiness and success are a destination. That if we just 'earn enough money', 'live in the right neighborhood' or 'get the man or woman of our dreams' then we will arrive at nirvana. The universe is always expanding and nothing in life is fixed in one place. The tree that stops growing new leaves is a dead tree. So, to assume that if we struggle hard enough we can arrive at a place where all the bad stuff stops and all the good stuff becomes permanent is illogical nonsense.

One of my bestselling books is called 'Alcohol Lied to Me' and it has helped tens of thousands of people to escape the trap of alcohol addiction. The single biggest problem I have with this book is many people are so desperate to stop drinking that they flick through the book looking for the 'answer', the reason why the book gets five star ratings. Often they are disappointed because there doesn't appear to be a magic bullet. People get back in control of their drinking by using this book, not by reading one magical concluding sentence on the last page but rather by walking a journey with me through the entire book. Just as in life, knowledge is absorbed through the journey we take. I am pretty sure that what you have learnt since you left school massively outweighs the information your teachers tried to pour into your head by having you remember facts verbatim.

Life is about the journey and I am here to tell you that you will never arrive at the end. This book is designed to profoundly change your life, just the way the knowledge I share in them changed mine. It took me forty years of struggling to swim upstream in life before I discovered the secrets in these books. I was an overweight, alcohol addicted angry man who never quite lived up to his own potential. I suffered depression, anxiety and low self esteem for many many years. No matter how much money I earned, no matter how much I drank, no matter how many things I bought, the vacuum inside me just kept growing bigger and bigger.

Since I discovered the material you are about to discover I have lost over sixty pounds in weight, quit drinking, given up my boring office job (to follow my dreams of being a full time author) and moved to a beautiful island in the Mediterranean that boasts three hundred days of sunshine a year. I am forty-one years old and these days I step out of my villa pick up my surfboard and spend the days on the beach with the girl of my dreams. Yes, I am insufferably annoying to be friends with on Facebook… and so will you be!

Forget all that 'positive thinking' nonsense and the get rich quick notions of the 'law of attraction' and other such new age bandwagon chasers. Yes, you can really have everything in life you want but I will warn you here and now! The chances are better than good that what you are really here to do, what that vacuum inside you needs to be filled with is a million miles away from what you currently think you need.

Before you start on the next chapter, I want you to prepare yourself for what comes next. Just as a building without foundations will not be habitable you cannot turn your life around and start manifesting your dreams with the click of your fingers. Books and gurus who claim that the Law of Attraction and 'Reality Creation' is easy are not telling the truth. Sure, on paper it may appear to be easy, but the same is true when I watch my mother bake and decorate a beautiful wedding cake. As I watch the icing and decorative piping almost will itself onto the cake it seems like the easiest thing to do in the world. However, I know that the flow, expertise and precision of my mother's hand has come from decades of doing this artwork over and over again. I don't need to attempt to replicate her work to know that it would be an abomination of a creation. Yes, in theory adopting the millionaire mindset is easy but this is only if you have changed your whole mindset and approach to life first – this part is not easy. What most people want is to get to the end of a book and then magically have a secret spell that will give them anything that they want the next day. If you are expecting this to happen I am afraid you have the wrong book, but worse than that – you will probably spend a lot of time and money trying to find something that does not exist.

There is an often-quoted saying 'thoughts become things', this is the cornerstone of books such as The Secret. The principle is simple; you get what you think about the most. So, if you think like a wealthy person you will become wealthy and so on. There is a slight problem with this theory and that is, it is completely wrong and doesn't work. Let me tell you why; thoughts are predominately generated by your ego (the insane part of you) but the ego doesn't have the power to manifest (or attract if you prefer). A thought in of itself is powerless, unless it becomes a belief. Essentially thoughts are conscious and beliefs are subconscious. For example you don't have to constantly remind yourself not to jump off tall buildings – you have a deeply embedded belief that this would be dangerous and most likely fatal behavior. Your subconscious protects you from the wild rambling desires of your ego by ignoring virtually everything it says. This is a very good thing – how many times have you caught yourself wishing harm to someone who has hurt you in some way (a cheating ex or a pressuring boss) only to calm down and realize violence wouldn't have helped. If your subconscious listened to every command of your ego the chances are you would be reading this from inside a prison cell, perhaps with me as your cellmate.

Before you begin the next chapter I would like you to spend a week doing something very important. I want you to become aware of your ego. It's imperative that you recognize where your desires and motivations are coming from. The reason we do this is to reduce the power of this part of you, to make space for you to hear the silence of your subconscious. In that silence is the answer to all of your most key questions, we just never stop to listen to what is waiting to be said. In fact most people go their entire lifetime without ever hearing the message that could have changed their life. The voice of the ego is so constant that we come to believe that this is who we are. The voice in our head passing judgment and demanding this or that is NOT who we are, it is an illusion.

But how do I know when my ego is speaking?

This is really simple – any thought or statement that begins with 'I' is the voice of your ego!

- *I drive a Mercedes.*
- *I will only ever stay in 5 star hotels.*
- *I won't accept people disrespecting me.*
- *I don't think she is good enough for him.*
- *I expect good service when I dine out.*
- *I deserve the promotion more than him.*

We all think we know who we are, but really most of the things that we decide to label ourselves with are purely statements of the ego. Even positive marques such as 'I am a great parent', 'I am a dedicated employee' or 'I am a loyal and reliable friend' – all these pronouncements come from a part of our mind that is unstable. The ego lives only in the conscious mind and every time you make a statement that begins with the word 'I', you can be sure it was created by some false belief in this part of your physical being.

All statements of 'I' are subjective and as such are pointless. Our body and mind are not who we are but rather just things we own for a short while. When people ask me what I do for a living I answer by saying 'I am an author'. But is that really who I am, I think not. The ego cannot cope having questions left unanswered and so we are forced to find comfort in applying a label to describe our reason to be. Then we become attached to this security blanket and set about embedding it deeper into our identification with life. Photographers get up each morning and take photographs – because that's what the label dictates. This is how we can spend an entire lifetime avoiding the point of life. Eventually we become so attached to the label that our ego tries to own it. We start to compete with other people who have selected the same direction as us. We need proof that we are the best, first, quickest or any illusionary piece of evidence that suggest we have achieved permanency in our label.

A person might proudly declare 'I give generously to charity, I am a good person'. We know this is pronouncement is the pointless bleating of the ego. Money is relative, if a billionaire makes a million dollar donation and at the same time a homeless man gives ten bucks, all the money he has – who is the more generous. The correct answer is neither, because any judgment on that is still just an assessment of the ego, which as I have already told you is insane!

All pain and suffering is created directly by this part of us and by our instance on laying claim to labels. On a personal level it can be felt in the sensation of jealously we experience when our neighbor pulls onto his driveway with a brand new sports car. On a global level it has been demonstrated countless times when nations declare war on each other. Mostly these acts of violence erupt when one country attempts to take something that another country has declared that it owns.

The ego is tiny and yet believes itself to be big and powerful. The subconscious is infinite but believes nothing at all. It feels no need to question or judge, it simply does.

We are prevented from consciously accessing this limitless and divine power because we can't be trusted not to act like complete power crazy, narcissistic idiots. Apart from that we would be likely to kill ourselves in seconds as the ego assures us that it knows what it is doing as it lifts the hood on the engine that beats our heart and fills our lungs with air. This is the same voice that assures us that we don't need to read the instruction manual when we buy a new piece of electronic equipment or flat pack furniture. I don't trust this voice any more than I trusted my friend at school who insisted that washing powder has the same effect as cocaine. He spent the afternoon in the hospital foaming from the nose.

We can only access the power of the subconscious by two very different methods. Firstly, it can be achieved through a lifetime of deep meditation and constant cleaning of the mind. Most people don't have the patience or dedication to take this route. However, the second route is practiced by us all and everyday. Repetition is how we fool the gatekeeper of the subconscious into allowing us access to this amazing super computer. The conscious mind is so limited that it can only complete one task at a time and so when we do something often enough the mind creates a physical pathway to complete this function automatically, thus freeing up processing power for other tasks. This would be a fantastic benefit of the human mind if we only did things that were founded in love and respect for ourselves and other people. For example if you started a routine of ringing your mother at 9am each morning and telling her that you love her. After a while you would not even have to think about it, at 9am you would gravitate towards the phone and start dialing even if you were thinking about doing something completely different.

Sadly we don't always tend to use this power for good. We prefer to repeatedly stick cigarettes in our mouth, eat junk food and drink alcohol until we feel ill. These are the programs that we allow to inadvertently bleed though into our subconscious. Once past the gatekeeper and inside there are no further filters to protect us, as this part of the mind does not judge or question, it only completes.

In the next chapter I am going to show you how to start listening to the power of your soul (or subconscious if you prefer). But much more than that I am going to show you how to pass commands over to this manifestation machine – once you learn how to do this your life is going to change. Not just a little, I am not talking about an unexpected cost of living increase at work or three numbers on the lottery. When this happens everything will change for the better. You will find true happiness, peace and purpose in your life. Abundance, wealth and love will be sucked towards you at such density that they will completely fill that aching vacuum at your core, this is an indescribable feeling – beyond your wildest dreams.

Before you can decide where you're going, how much money you want, how much happiness you want, you need to be aware of where you are. If you are lost, giving you a map is absolutely useless unless you know exactly where you currently are. Then you can plan where you're going to go.

So I would like you to take a piece of paper. Please write down at the top of the piece of paper your current salary. How much money you earn, everything included, per year. Write it down in big letters at the top of the page. Underneath it in bigger letters I would like you to write down how much you want to be earning one year from now. Be positive; make it a stretch for yourself. If you currently earn $40,000 a year, putting down $45,000 for next year is not good enough. It's not a big enough leap. If you're on $40,000 a year at the moment, I would suggest you write down $70,000 for this time next year.

If you're on $70,000 a year, put $125,000, if you're on $150,000, put $250,000. Make it a stretch. Then under that write down how much you want to be earning five years from now. Imagine what you can do with that money.

Good. So in front of you, you should have three figures. You should have your current salary looking all tiny at the top there. You should have your one year goal and your outrageous five year goal. By the way if you are looking at it and it doesn't feel a little bit crazy and impossible then it's too small. Next, I want you to write down what you are going to do with the money. You see virtually everybody wants to be rich but if you ask most people why they want that they shrug and say something like 'I don't know, I just do'. If you can't answer the 'why' then you don't have enough clarity on the situation. Paint a vivid, colorful picture of what your life looks like when you hit that amazing five year goal. What car are you driving, how is your relationships, where do you live and where are you vacationing. It doesn't have to be material stuff, perhaps you have aspirations to be the biggest donor at your church or you want to use the freedom that wealth gives you to volunteer for a charity that is close to your heart. It doesn't matter what it is, so long as you can make a clear statement of intent.

What I would like you to do every day for 21 days, first thing in the morning - put a pad by the bed if you want. When you get up, do this. Or maybe you have a pad in the car, you write it before you start your journey, or maybe you have a pad on your desk at work and it's the first thing you do every morning when you get into work. I want you to write down, I earn and then put in your one year goal.

So if you're currently on $50,000 a year and your goal is to reach $85,000, write down every morning, I earn $85,000 per year. When you write something down, you're absolutely forced to concentrate on the message. This is just a small act but it will slowly, minutely alter your subconscious programming. Your beliefs about how much you earn.

If you do it every day the message builds stronger and stronger and stronger. Even the worst salesman in the world knows that repetition sells. It works on the subconscious mind too. This simple action will make a massive difference over time to your life. If you haven't done it - if you were driving earlier and you did not write down your financial goals, stop reading and do it now.

Finally I want you to take that goal amount and write it down again BUT with an extra zero on the end of it. That may seem crazy or just downright impossible but it is better to aim for the stars and only hit the moon. Most people are not aiming any further than the ceiling above their head. Be one of the crazy ones who dares to dream big and you should trust me on this, amazing things will happen!

I will close this chapter with a little story. Once upon a time there was a couple that had achieved many of their ambitions in life, yet there was one main goal outstanding: They wanted to swim to Japan. They reflected on this goal for a long time and one day they set off. They were not used to swimming so they found it difficult. They were aware of how heavy their limbs felt. They ached with the constant effort, especially when the strong current was against them.

Gradually, however, their bodies got used to swimming and they developed a style that became effortless and rhythmical. They began to notice the water around them, for example how it changed color as the days went by. In the early morning it would be clear and blue and in certain lights it sparkled emerald green. As the sun set it developed the rich warm colors of the evening sky. And they became aware of the creatures in the water, the small silver fish that swam with them in the day, the dark shadows that skimmed by them in the deep. They became aware of how the sound of the waves changed as the water lapped their ears and they felt the subtle changes of the weather as breezes turned into winds and died down again. They learned how to find food in the water, how to nourish themselves, and how to use their bodies effortlessly. They developed a refined sense of smell so that they could detect changes in the environment by the scent carried to them on the breeze.

They swam for days and weeks with no sight of land. One day they saw the dark profile of land on the horizon. They swam on and they recognized the shoreline of Japan. As they approached they became quiet and eventually they looked at each other and they knew. At that moment they turned back to the sea and swam on.

Freedom From The Good Opinions Of Others

"Throughout human history, in any great endeavor requiring the common effort of many nations and men and women everywhere, we have learned - it is only through seriousness of purpose and persistence that we ultimately carry the day. We might liken it to riding a bicycle. You stay upright and move forward so long as you keep up the momentum", Ban Ki-moon

It doesn't matter how much passion and focus you have for your endeavors, other people are going to try and derail your attempts to enter the 20%, or perhaps a better way to put that is 'to try and prevent you leaving the 80%'. You may wonder why people who love and care about you would do that, and the answer is many fold. For the most part they just can't see the vision and possibilities the way you can. Sometimes they sense the risk you are taking and their negative comments are more a reflection of their own fear than anything else. But there is another reason and it is entirely subconscious.

In my books on stopping drinking I advise my readers not to hang around their old drinking buddies any more because I know for sure they will do their best to get that newly sober person back drinking again. The reason is deep down inside all problem drinkers know that what they are doing is harmful and must eventually stop one way or another. Of course in their conscious mind they are replaying the marketing messages that state that alcohol is just a harmless social pleasantry, something to make good times better, the reason for and maker of any social occasion. However, in their subconscious mind they know they are addicted to a drug, a drug that wants to kill them. So when a drinking friend comes along and announces that he or she has given up the booze, it causes them psychological pain.

Human beings are motivated only by two forces, the need to gain pleasure and avoid pain. When someone appears to be raising their standards above your own it causes pain by association. The correlation of their action must mean the drinker is now relegated to a position that is beneath the non-drinker. The drinker has only two ways to respond to the pain and fear. They can also stop drinking and move toward pleasure or they can move away from the thing causing the pain. As they are unlikely to dump the sober friend just because they stopped drinking, they are left with only one option... to encourage their friend to start drinking again.

The same is true when people around you sense that you have raised your game and you appear to be thinking and acting differently to most people. There is a very real, albeit unconscious fear that you may actually succeed. If you achieve success and actually become wealthy, leaving behind your friends, who remain struggling in the 80%. Then this action on your part will cause them a double dose of psychological pain. Firstly your high standards will highlight their own low standards and also you will steal all their excuses. How can they continue to explain away their poverty by saying only the corrupt get rich, only the people with a better education or only people from a better part of town get rich if their friend managed to do it.

When you get started on this and you tell people about your plans and goals be prepared for them to tell you all sorts of negative stuff. They will tell you that it's impossible, they will tell you horror stories about people they know who tried the same thing and they lost everything. They will piss all over your grand plans and they will do it sure in the knowledge that they are only doing it because they care about you and don't want you to get hurt. It is because you will get this advice directly from your loved ones just as much as your acquaintances that I title this chapter 'Freedom from the GOOD opinions of others'. My advice to you is listen to your heart, if your heart says do it then trust the voice inside you. The very worst thing that can happen is you will fail and learn a valuable lesson.

Don't concentrate on the word 'fail' in that sentence, focus on the word 'valuable'. Remember Thomas Edison failed to invent the electric light bulb over a thousand times. With each failure he learnt another lesson, until he had the sufficient knowledge to succeed. Seriously, show me a successful, wealthy man and I will show you a person who has failed countless times. I am personally proud to have failed more times than I can recall but that doesn't mean I have found a way to enjoy it or not let it upset me deeply. I can tell you that I have on many occasions in the past got to the point where I thought to myself 'you've really messed up this time Craig, your not getting out of this is one piece'. But despite my prophecies of doom and gloom I always do come out the other side, a little bit wiser and with a few more grey hairs – you will do the same.

It's okay to fail and it's okay to be afraid. Most people will back away from opportunities when they feel that strong sensation of fear. We are more used to seeing fear as a warning sign that we should listen to, and not a green light for what we are planning. When we use the word fear we normally apply it to situations where we wrongly or rightly predict that we are at risk of harm. For example standing on the edge of a tall building generates a sensation of fear and anxiety so we become acutely aware of what could happen if we act inappropriately in those situations. We can be afraid before a job interview because we have become attached to an outcome and don't want to experience rejection followed by the loss of that outcome. However, fear isn't always this obvious or dramatic but it can still be hugely limiting in our life.

When people go on a diet they start out with good intentions and a desperate desire to improve the way they look and feel. An honorable pursuit, but why do nearly 95% of them not only end up putting back on all the weight they lost plus and additional few pounds for good measure? The answer is fear, at the start of the diet the pain of looking in the mirror or not being able to squeeze into their favorite denim any more creates low level fear. For example 'what if I just keep getting bigger', 'what if I have nothing to wear at the party', 'what if they start calling me names at school' etc. So, we start the diet motivated to move our chubby body away from the fear. Then we lose a bit of weight and the original fear subsides but it is often replaced by a new concern. You see, we enjoy our tasty treats and takeaways in front of a good movie. Suddenly we feel like we are depriving ourselves of some of the fun bits of life. We fear that if we carry on being strict with ourselves we are going to be short changed by life and have less fun. Thus begins the yo-yo diet routine that dominates the life of so many.

I am writing this section of the book in the business class cabin of another British Airways flight and even here fear is present. I am not talking about worrying about the plane crashing or running into some scary turbulence. I have been on board for just two hours and so far I have been offered free alcohol at least half a dozen times. I can't drink alcohol because it has a nasty habit of trying to kill me. If you have read my book *Alcohol Lied to Me* you will know that I had a near two decade long battle with the booze and I became teetotal about six or seven years ago. I don't have to struggle to stay away from drinking, no part of me wants to go back where I was but there is an element of fear at the back of my head every time the airhostess comes down the aisle with the drinks trolley and I turn down a very expensive French Bordeaux and instead ask for a cheap glass of water. The frugal northerner in me feels like I am getting ripped off – I feel like I am getting much poorer value for money than the guy next to me who has so far knocked back $100 worth of wine and brandy. I am 99% certain that I won't buckle in the name of value but I am acutely aware and afraid of that 1% that still lingers at the back of my mind.

Fear is present on a daily basis and in a myriad of ways. We are taught to be careful, to listen to fear and respond accordingly and the vast majority of society obeys this unwritten law. The result is a safer, more boring & less fulfilling life. This is the world of the Average Joe and the Average Jane – safe and steady but beige. What I am encouraging you to do is respond to fear in a highly counter intuitive way. Instead of seeing fear as a warning I want you to see it as an opportunity light blinking on the dashboard of your life. Essentially, if you are afraid of it then you must do it!

Fear Response Examples

Situation	Average Joe Response	Fearless Response
Afraid of drinking alcohol.	Path of least resistance. Surely just one won't hurt will it?	Take the least easy path. See it as a clear sign that drinking won't serve you.
Afraid to get started on your business idea.	Put it off until the timing is better. AKA Never get staretd	Commit and commit hard. Jump in at the deep end and start swimming.
Afraid to go through	Cancel for	Fear means

with the charity parachute jump.	'health reasons' explains to friends they would love to but the doctor said no.	there is no other option but to do the jump. Everything else will make their comfort zone contract.

I can't begin to tell you how many people I meet who are full of regret, and virtually never about the things they have done in their life but much more commonly about the things they never did. The last time I saw my aunty Angela she was having a coffee with my parents at their home in Darlington. I joined them all for a short while and as I sat down Angela was expressing her regret that she had never learned to drive. She had started to learn but got too afraid to ever put in for the test and it just became one of those things we label shoulda, woulda, coulda. Two years previously Angela had sadly been diagnosed with C.U.P. cancer (cancer of unknown primary origin). She was still her old lively self but her prognosis was not great, all treatment had ultimately failed. The doctors estimated she had between six and nine months to live. Angela decided that before it became impossible she was going to take and pass her driving test.

She never got the chance as she died three weeks later. The moment she died passing or failing that driving test became irrelevant; all the fear about taking the test in the first place also became equally as irrelevant. There are dozens of things that you want in life that you don't have because fear is preventing you going after them. One day in the future all that fear will be rendered pointless by the same event that Angela went through, the event that nobody has ever managed to avoid. What I am saying is that your ego is trying to protect you from harm by encouraging you to avoid risk by using fear as a virtual 10x4 to hit you about the head with.

Your body is like an apartment shared between two tenants. The ego and the soul, or if you prefer the conscious mind and the unconscious mind are the tenants of your body. The soul is eternal and divine, it is essentially a fragment of God and it knows this for certain. It is also acutely aware that the apartment it is renting is temporary and when the lease ends it will just move to a new place and start over. However, the ego knows that when the lease ends that's the end of the story, its game over. This creates a sensation of blind panic for the ego, which point blank refuses to accept the situation. It kicks and screams trying to prove that it can prevent the lease from ending. Hey perhaps if you fill the apartment with more and more stuff and never leave so they can't come in and dump your possessions then perhaps the lease will continue evermore right? The ego is so terrified of the end it has been rendered insane by the constant thought of it.

Out of this insanity we get all the self-limiting beliefs that hold us back.

- Save for a rainy day
- What can go wrong, will go wrong

- I need the security of my job (that I hate).
- You are not ready for your driving test.
- You are not good enough for that promotion at work

The ego uses the past as a reverse projector in an attempt to control the uncontrollable. Fear is liberally applied to all areas of your life in the hope that it will keep you safe if completely unfulfilled. You are alive but miserable, that's good enough. The ego doesn't particularly care how happy you are, its primary focus is trying in vain to avoid the inevitable final act, at whatever cost.

What I am about to ask you to do is acknowledge that one of your tenants is insane and while you can't evict you can decide to stop listening to his/her insane ramblings. From this point on fear should be seen as the screams in the night of your troublesome tenant. All the predictions of doom, gloom, terror and trauma are nothing more than a desperate illusion.

Start living in the knowledge that the only moment that exists is this one, right here and right now. The past and the future do not exist and they never will – this is it and this is all there will ever be.

There is a percentage chance that this nineteen year old Boeing 777-200 aircraft will crash before I reach my final destination – should I just stop writing now just in case? No of course not, because right here in this moment I am alive and as long as that situation continues I have a message to get out there.

Exercise:

I want you to stop reading at this point and take a little life inventory. Grab a pen and paper and write down everything you can think of that you have wanted to achieve but have been prevented doing so by fear. Perhaps you have always wanted to skydive but can't quite bring yourself to sign up for a jump. Maybe there is a senior position opening at work and you have told yourself that you are not quite ready and maybe try again in a few years. Perhaps you have been head over heals in love with Nicola on reception for years and never done anything about it?

On a blank piece of paper draw four columns, in the first column write your goal, in the second write down how fear is preventing you from achieving this goal, in the third column write down what will happen if you continue to let fear dominate this area of your life and in the final column I want you to imagine how you would feel if you ignored the 'Danger Do Not Pass' signs hanging on the wall of your comfort zone and charged on through regardless.

Example:

Goal	Fear	Failure	Success
To skydive	I might die, or worse I	It will always be there as	I will feel invincible. I

| | might embarrass myself by refusing to jump! | something that says 'you are a coward'. | will have done something most people would never be brave enough to do. I would feel huge pride in myself. |

Zig Ziglar would describe the start of his day in such a beautiful way. He used to say 'every morning at 6am my opportunity clock would go off and wake me up. I don't call it an alarm clock because that's negative. That bell signals the start of a whole new day full of wonderful opportunities'.

As ever I want this to be a practical investment of your time and money, something that you can take and implement quickly into your life and consequently see massive positive change as a result. I am going to close this chapter on fear with a challenge, for you to do one thing right now that fear has been making you avoid. It could be something as simple as picking up the phone and apologizing to someone you didn't act in the right way with. It could be clicking send on a resignation email or a job application form – find something that you are afraid of and embrace it as an opportunity

An Attitude Of Gratitude

Have an attitude of gratitude. This is a popular and perhaps over pronounced statement, but one can never underestimate the power behind these words. Many people who first come into contact with the Law Of Attraction hear that in order to attract something you want you must act like you already have it. To give thanks as though that new car or lottery win is already in your possession.

As we have already discovered; your conscious desires and wants are an irrelevance, so forget about what you think you want. These dreams are all in the tomorrow and none of your business. Concentrate on what is in your life today, this moment and be grateful for it. Even problems present as an opportunity for love and gratitude. Give your problems to God, ask God to erase them and then give thanks for that.

I think Marelisa Fabrega describes it best in her change blog when she says:

Gratitude means thankfulness, counting your blessings, noticing simple pleasures, and acknowledging everything that you receive. It means learning to live your life as if everything were a miracle, and being aware on a continuous basis of how much you've been given. Gratitude shifts your focus from what your life lacks to the abundance that is already present. In addition, behavioral and psychological research has shown the surprising life improvements that can stem from the practice of gratitude. Giving thanks makes people happier and more resilient, it strengthens relationships, it improves health, and it reduces stress.

Two psychologists, Michael McCollough of Southern Methodist University in Dallas, Texas, and Robert Emmons of the University of California at Davis, wrote an article about an experiment they conducted on gratitude and its impact on well-being. The study split several hundred people into three different groups and all of the participants were asked to keep daily diaries. The first group kept a diary of the events that occurred during the day without being told specifically to write about either good or bad things; the second group was told to record their unpleasant experiences; and the last group was instructed to make a daily list of things for which they were grateful. The results of the study indicated that daily gratitude exercises resulted in higher reported levels of alertness, enthusiasm, determination, optimism, and energy. In addition, those in the gratitude group experienced less depression and stress, were more likely to help others, exercised more regularly, and made greater progress toward achieving personal goals.

People tend to take for granted the good that is already present in their lives. There's a gratitude exercise that instructs that you should imagine losing some of the things that you take for granted, such as your home, your ability to see or hear, your ability to walk, or anything that currently gives you comfort. Then imagine getting each of these things back, one by one, and consider how grateful you would be for each and every one. In addition, you need to start finding joy in the small things instead of holding out for big achievements such as getting the promotion, having a comfortable nest egg saved up, getting married, having the baby, and so on–before allowing yourself to feel gratitude and joy.

Another way to use giving thanks to appreciate life more fully is to use gratitude to help you put things in their proper perspective. When things don't go your way, remember that every difficulty carries within it the seeds of an equal or greater benefit. In the face of adversity ask yourself: "What's good about this?", "What can I learn from this?", and "How can I benefit from this?"
Once you become oriented toward looking for things to be grateful for, you will find that you begin to appreciate simple pleasures and things that you previously took for granted. Gratitude should not be just a reaction to getting what you want, but an all-the-time gratitude, the kind where you notice the little things and where you constantly look for the good even in unpleasant situations. Today, start bringing gratitude to your experiences, instead of waiting for a positive experience in order to feel grateful; in this way, you'll be on your way toward becoming a master of gratitude.

If you live by the principles of this book for the next 21 days I guarantee you will start to witness miracles. Start right now, be grateful for everything in your life right now in this moment. Keep a gratitude journal on your desk or by your bed. Start and end each day with a huge list of how wonderful your life is and you will be amazed at what happens.

I don't just need you to do this in the good times but it is even more important that you do it in the dark times. When life seems not worth living, when you are down on your luck pick up the pen and be grateful for the good things.

I tell you nothing here that I don't do myself and I will admit that I am no saint and I do have to wear a reminder to ensure that I constantly live in a state of gratitude for my life in this moment. I have never found wearing jewelry comfortable and so I don't own any necklaces, rings or other decorative adornments I don't even wear a watch for the same reason. However, around my left wrist I do wear a simple cotton string. It is there for one reason, when I look at it I automatically say the words 'everything in this moment is perfect'.

When I finally give up playing the character 'Craig Beck' and give up on this body and shuffle off the stage I think they should engrave my tombstone with 'Everything in this moment is just perfect'!

Have you noticed how much hatred some people harbor for rich people? If you ever get the opportunity to lease a luxury car take note of the change in attitude other drivers have towards you. I guarantee you will get cut up more and let out of junctions much less. You may even park up and on your return find someone has spat on your car or worse. People in the 80% are wracked with envy and jealousy and this is just another reason why they will never leave the gang at the bottom of the hill. How can you hate something you want to achieve and still hope to achieve it? This sort of thinking creates civil war in your brain and it is a battle that will always come down on the side of the negative.

The reason the negative view always wins is simple. Yes, these people consciously want to be rich but subconsciously they hate rich people. If the two sections of our mind were equally balanced then perhaps it could go either way. Unfortunately, imagine your subconscious is a billion dollar thoroughbred racehorse. By comparison your conscious mind is a three legged blind donkey. These envious folks don't have a hope of winning this battle and getting the outcome they claim they want. They will get the outcome generated by their beliefs, which reside within the significantly more powerful part of their brain.

Millionaire University – Gratitude Key Learning Point

"If the only prayer you say in your life is "thank you," that would suffice.", Meister Eckhart

Are you thankful for what you have in your life?

Do you recognize that on a daily basis when you get up in the morning?

You need to. Do you realize that the Millionaire Mindset always incorporates a grateful outlook? And this state of mind does not begin after the wealth has arrived but beforehand.

By intentionally applying the Millionaire's Law of Gratitude, you act as though the Universe or divinity, depending how you see it, exists to provide what you really want, when you ask for it. You believe that you are worthy of what you get, regardless of what it is you get. You connect to what you have and behave commensurate to it.

Individuals who are without this sort of ongoing appreciation constantly end up poor, living in scarcity or not getting the life-style they want to have. These people are the 80% that I refer to constantly throughout this course. They regard themselves as lower on the totem pole of life and question why they can't ever be greater than what they are. The main explanation for this is that they are short of acknowledgment to what they desire and do not show to the Cosmos what they desire or deserve to have.

There is no question that you acquire what you call for and you get it in great quantity when you put a great deal of energy into it. By demonstrating thankfulness, you are demonstrating that the energy you exert accorded to exactly what you wanted; and you will get more of that you want.

You can explain to individuals by what they have and by what they get just by observing them and taking a look at how they dress, walk, and act. You can often tell if they have thankfulness by the way they show themselves.

This is why whenever you examine the habits of truly wealthy individuals; you discover these people get wealthier. They have a personal debt of thankfulness and show it daily. By doing this, they are informing the cosmos that they are thankful they have all these resources and deserve them. The universe reacts by providing even more.

If an individual does have wealth but does not display appreciation, he or she will ultimately exhaust it. This is due to the fact that he or she is saying to the cosmos that they does not deserve it. When the cosmos identifies this, the cosmos stops providing.

However, if an individual does not have wealth but shows gratitude for what he or she has, the universe will notice that and will consequently give the particular person more of what that individual desires. By doing this, that particular person does not remain in scarcity for a long time.

If a man or woman is short of wealth and does not present thankfulness, he or she will continue to tolerate scarcity because they has not displayed they have the right to even more.

This is the reason that when we display thankfulness, we are nearer to Divine being or the Cosmos than anybody else. And we get the compensations for doing this. For that reason, the more thankful we are when we get assets, the more assets we will obtain. And sometimes, these benefits will begin occurring even more quickly than in the past. As you develop new beliefs and behave peacefully those thought and feelings with a display of appreciation for possessing those beliefs, the more you will be to getting that of which you believed or ask for.

Gratitude has many advantages in that it can keep you from feeling insufficient. It can help keep your thoughts concentrated on the great instead of the negative. You can feel more abundantly by offering thankfulness. This is exactly why you should abide by the Law of Gratitude if you really want what you pursue.

Consider this. If your display of appreciation is powerful, the consequences that return to you will be substantial. If your personal debt of appreciation is continual, your accumulation will also be continual. If you begin reducing your perspective of thankfulness, you will discover you will fall farther behind dramatically and wind up on the losing end of life. This is the reason that possessing appreciation is so vital. It is so vital that it was made into one of the universal ordinances.

If you imagine it, with no thankfulness, there is a missing link somewhere in our existences. We understand that a little something ought to be there, but may not recognize it until a person points it out. The reality is that declaring, "thanks" for what you receive is a significant step to getting a kind of gratitude. But this isn't all there is about the Millionaire's Law of Gratitude. Actually, there is an excellent interpretation of this law that states, "If you are to acquire the wealth and benefits you pursue, it is important that you must act upon and abide by this law." This suggests that if you do not follow the Millionaire's Law of Gratitude, you will never get the abundant lifestyle that you really want. It is that straightforward.

Besides being thankful for what you get, what is the precise manner in which the Millionaire's Law of Gratitude functions?

It may be explained as a normal concept that action and counteraction are alike and also contrary in direction at the same time. This suggests that anything we put our awareness or emotive power toward can be desirable or harmful for us. And this power will at some point appear in our existences. This is among the concepts you must recognize and learn about if you are serious about entering the 20%.

Neither the cosmos nor our subconscious mind labels things as being good or bad. The two elements are handled the same. In this concern, what we put our concentration on is what we get back.

Good and bad things do not happen, stuff happens – it's as simple as that. To become rich you need to be grateful for the stuff, all of it. Not just the 'stuff' that you subjectively single out as being 'good'.

The significance here is on applying affirmative power out to the world. By doing this, we are paying attention to what we desire and not on what we do not desire. You may not understand this, but gratitude is extremely effective. It has a great deal of high-energy beneficial resonance of thought. This is why I pointed out above that possessing appreciation connects you to the Cosmos or Divinity, according to how you view it.

In the absence of gratitude, you have no energy, because they both link up side by side. And by utilizing our thoughts for constructive traits, we are in truth utilizing the potential we have to manufacture the real world we yearn for. So when we show thankfulness, we are in reality creating superior energy affirmative resonances of thought. This strong vitality can only result in a single manifestation-- great success.

Whenever you do anything in life, you present the thankfulness to make it perform. If you establish objectives for yourself, you ought to show thankfulness for having achieved the objectives you set down. When you do write your intentions down, think about them as having been previously obtained and be thankful for receiving them. Your thankfulness will be so potent, so stimulating, that all the individuals around you can't help but recognize that about your character.

Those who are not prosperous or do not get what they want in life are in truth experts at driving away the financial success they want so badly. They break the universal code of gratitude. This is similar to kicking your boss in the ass and expecting a pay rise as the outcome of your action.

As a matter of fact, there are 5 crucial oversights or means of thinking that the 80% make with appreciation and gratitude that results in them not getting the level of wealth that they really want in life.

These 5 ways consist of:

1. **Wealth Scarcity Assumptions:**

    Some people question if there is sufficient to go around for everybody. If your mindset that the cosmos has only a finite inventory, you are going nowhere in life and will never ever develop into anything. This is a significant misconception in life. In reality, there is sufficient wealth in the world. It is unlimited. Divinity guaranteed us that we would have wealth endlessly if we decided to possess it. The world is energy. Energy is endless. Consequently, what we desire emerges from energy. It only goes to prove that the world will never lack anything we really want. It will consistently offer us with what we desire when we desire it. We simply need to ask.

2. **Non-resistance to what is:**

This is an unfounded notion or fundamental that a lot of people have. It keeps us from possessing the thankfulness we need to have. When we presume with non-resistance, we are in truth getting the attitude that whatever takes place, takes place. We don't battle with the events of life, we just let it be. In other words, men and women who feel this way assume they are worthy of what they obtained or strongly believe that was the way it was meant to be.

Consequently, they confine themselves to what daily life has to give. If it consists of a thing they can't do anything about, they just let it be and claim that is the way it was determined to be. In this particular case, you can use the law of opposites and believe that there is good in the predicament rather than negative.

3. **Failing to find their purpose:**

A lot of people have the tendency to link contentment with being happy and having wealth. But there is a distinction. When you are content, you take what is. You can be contented without being thankful. This is due to the fact that you accepted factors exactly the way they are and you did not dispute them or battle against reality.

Happiness, alternatively, is a condition of pleasure or thankfulness. It is an extremely favorable and desirable psychological fuel. By being contented, you are really restricting yourself to what you can have in your life. It is essential to be more than happy and completely satisfied now. It you do, you will have thankfulness and will be in the stance for much wealth.

4. **Amnesty:**

You may not know this but forgiveness is also an aspect of the Millionaire's Law of Gratitude. This indicates you have to absolve anybody who did negative things to you previously as well as in the present, along with in the future. This is particularly important if you have a dislike against somebody for a very long time. The technique you know you forgive them is by asking yourself if you can either wish them well or be thankful for them. If you can honestly answer "absolutely," you have without a doubt absolved them.

Amnesty is so crucial to our aspirations in life that if we do not do it and keep any animosity, worry, or any irritation inside, it can truly impede us from acquiring what we desire in life. Finally, we should learn how to absolve our own selves for what we do to other people and our own selves. If we can examine ourselves in the mirror and say we love ourselves, we are on our way to experiencing the lifestyle we desire.

5. **Cease over-thinking:**

Sadly, many intelligent people are cursed by the power of their own brain. These people would like to refrain from thinking after they get a thought in their mind. I used to drink two bottles of wine a day to try and shut off my thinking mind. This I don't recommend unless you are happy with death being the solution to your overthinking.

The problem for people in the 80% is they do not harness the power of their mind. They do not intend to surpass thinking and actually act upon the things they think about. They go into the procedures of considering, pondering and planning, but they never take action and follow up on what they feel.

If you want broad based prosperity in your life as well as wealth, you will follow these edicts and when you do, you can get whatever you desire in life and be content accomplishing it.

The Ten Actions of The Super Rich

"Success is not the key to happiness. Happiness is the key to success. If you love what you are doing, you will be successful", Albert Schweitzer

We have a crazy situation at the moment in the world, especially in the United States. Donald Trump won the election preaching and anti-immigration message. Does it not seem bizarre that a nation built on immigration would choose to demonize and vote against immigrants? We have the same problem in the United Kingdom, with particular anger being vented in the direction of the Polish people who have arrived in large numbers. Over the past few decades' employers of manual labor in the UK have had a problem, they couldn't find enough people willing to get their hands dirty and do the work. Unbelievably, long term unemployed folk, living hand to mouth on state benefits consider manual labor beneath them! Such is the sense of entitlement that we have created, that they would rather live in poverty and spend their energy looking for someone to blame for their situation than they would just roll up their sleeves and take action.

The message has been sent out *'you are entitled to the very best, don't accept anything less that that. If you can't afford it then put it on credit – why should you go without'*? So poor unemployed British people sit at home in front of a giant flat screen TV watching their two hundred channels of satellite subscription, while paying the minimum payment on their ever-expanding credit card. They won't work and they refuse to accept the reality.

Then along comes an immigrant from a country where poverty means poverty. Forget not having a big TV, we are talking about not even having enough food to eat. No decent healthcare, no prospects, no free handouts – nothing! A lot of these people have lived through communist regimes and revolutions – they have seen and experienced the very worst of humanity. Back home, even if they wanted to dig the soil to earn a little money, the opportunities simply are not there. When an immigrant lands in the United States or the United Kingdom they can't believe what they see. A land of opportunity and possibility awaits them. They get offered a job, so it's only paying five pounds an hour and it means working hard in a field digging up potatoes for eight hours a day but it's gold dust compared to what they left behind. The immigrants are grateful for the work and they have no problem putting their backs into what they do and working hard for the opportunity.

While the entitled folk look down on the work and declare that it is beneath them, the immigrant calls home and says 'Wow this place is amazing! There are plenty of jobs available. I have money in my pocket, somewhere to sleep and I even get a day off. You should come here too'. The friends and family of the worker jump on a plane and come to join him. It is at this point that the entitled start to complain that these bloody immigrants are coming over and stealing all the jobs. The mentality of these people is so poor is they even feel entitled to the jobs that they have previously refused to do.

Becoming rich is not an overnight journey, it's not easy and it does require hard work and passion. Anyone who tells you otherwise either knows a lot more about this stuff than me or they are selling snake oil. I am asking you to trust me on this because I know you would rather be rich than right! After all, doing it your way has only brought you to the position you are in right now. I am going to suggest some dramatic changes, and I won't lie to you – some of them are going to make you uncomfortable for a while. Remember, your comfort zone is a beautiful place but nothing ever grows there. So try to embrace the uncomfortable and enjoy the knowledge that it is expanding your financial potential.

If you currently don't have as much money as you want, then it is a clear sign that your comfort zone is too small. The state of your financial health is directly related to the size of your comfort zone. The only way to expand your comfort zone is to charge up to the edge of it and when you see the warning signs that are nailed to the walls. Signs that say DANGER – Extreme Discomfort – Do Not Pass. Instead of turning back around like everyone else in the 80% you smash through the wall and embrace the pain that comes with it. Every time you do this the boundary of your comfort zone is moved outward to the new point you have reached.

But what do I mean by smash through the walls of your comfort zone. I mean do things that scare you and do them often. Go for the job that you don't think you are good enough to get, invest in the training course you have been putting off, get stared with that business that you have always wanted to do, do a charity skydive, approach the beautiful woman you pass everyday on the way to work and ask her for a date. I don't care what you do, as long as it scares you and makes you feel uncomfortable.

I am hoping you are thinking, yes Craig I can do that! Good, but that's only **Action Point One**. Expanding your comfort zone is an ethereal challenge but I always want you to make a tangible and practical changes to your life. **Action Point Two** of the millionaire mindset starts with a commitment that from this moment forward nothing goes on credit. I want you to cut off your own line of credit, right here and now. Go grab a pair of scissors and cut up the Amex and the credit cards. If you can't afford to buy it in cash then you can't afford to buy it, period! Stop falling for the entitlement bullshit that you deserve everything you want. You don't and feeding your ego with purchases on credit is the fast track to a life of scarcity.

Ask yourself how much thought to do you put into buying a can of soda? Do you worry if you can really afford it? Do you spend a lot of time agonizing about the cost implications of buying it? Almost certainly not, you buy the can and that's that – it's not a big deal because it's only an insignificant amount of money to you. When a millionaire goes to buy a sports car this is how he feels.

You can use this observation as a yardstick as to whether you can really afford things or not. If you find yourself wondering 'can I afford this' then the chances are good that you can't and you should walk on by.

For the most part it is the non-millionaires who are obsessed with looking wealthy. I have a friend called Graham, he is an engineer and he lives with his wife Emma in a nice four bedroom detached house in suburbia. On their drive they have a new BMW and next to it a sporty ex demo Porsche for Emma to drive. If you meet Graham he will show you around his wine cellar, treat you to an amazing meal and let you try on his new Rolex watch. Everything you see is an illusion, an illusion that feels so vivid and real to Graham and Emma that they can no longer see what is in front of their nose. Both of the cars are leased, the house is mortgaged and the Rolex went on the credit card under the justification that he deserved something special for his fortieth last year. Graham believes that he is rich, but simply losing his job would reveal the reality in less than a couple of months.

Your choice of home — and how often you choose a new one — will determine your ability to accumulate wealth. According to The Millionaire Next Door, that wealthy family has been next door for quite a while. Half of millionaires have lived in the same house for more than 20 years.

In Stop Acting Rich, Thomas Stanley digs deeper into how your address affects your spending, writing:

Nothing has a greater impact on your wealth and your consumption than your choices of house and neighborhood. If you live in a high-price home in an exclusive community, you will spend more than you should and your ability to save and build wealth will be compromised.... People who live in million-dollar homes are not millionaires. They may be high-income producers but, by trying to emulate glittering rich millionaires, they are living a treadmill existence.

He cites several statistics to back this up, including: Ninety percent of millionaires live in homes valued below $1 million; 28.3% live in homes valued at $300,000 or less. On average, millionaires have a mortgage that is less than one-third of the value of their homes.

If you really want to reduce your housing bill, join the 67,000 millionaires who live in mobile homes.
If you're looking to buy a home, Stanley provides this advice: "The market value of the home you purchase should be less than three times your household's total annual realized income."

The majority of millionaires own their cars, rather than lease. Approximately a quarter have a current-year model, but another quarter drive a car that is four years old or older. More than a third tend to buy used vehicles. What is the most popular car maker among millionaires, according to Stop Acting Rich? Toyota.

So who's driving all those BMWs and Mercedes? Not millionaires. Eighty-six percent of "prestige/luxury" cars are bought by non-millionaires. In fact, Stanley writes that "one in three people who traded in their old car for a new one were upside down and owed more on the trade-in than its market value." It's tough to get wealthy doing stuff like that.

"Stop buying things you don't need, to impress people you don't even like." – Suze Orman

Action Point Three: You need to start paying yourself first, at the moment the chances are good that the only person you are paying first is the IRS. Before you even get to the money you have earned the taxman has been there first and there is a very good reason he does this. Most people live in a world where the months are too long to fit the money we have available. The taxman wants paying before you get to the point in the month where you have to tighten your belt. You need to set up an automatic payment that will leave your account the very same day you get paid. This should be put into a savings account that you have limited access to. The sort of account whereby if your child needs an emergency operation then you could access the funds but with enough penalties and incentives to keep the money untouched that if you get the urge to upgrade the TV then you will find that it is not worth your while to withdraw the money.

Ideally you should be aiming to pay yourself 15% to 30% before you get anywhere near your salary. However, I do appreciate that if you are currently struggling to make ends meet then that suggestion won't seem very doable at the moment. Even if you can only currently afford to save 1% of your income, then do it! This is one of the key habits of millionaires and the super rich. Start small if you have to but do start now.

Action Point Four: Be careful about small expenses
All of us are usually careful about making big investments and huge purchases. However, we tend to spend recklessly on seemingly small expenses.

But of course, these small expenses can amass to a big amount.

As Suze Orman rightly points out, "Look everywhere you can to cut a little bit from your expenses. It will all add up to a meaningful sum."

Action Point Five: Focus on the future - It is very easy to spend money for getting something that we like but at the end of the day, you will end up spending everything no matter how well you earn. Shift your focus to the future instead of getting satisfaction in the present.

"You can be young without money, but you can't be old without it." – Tennessee Williams

Action Point Six: Put things in black and white - There are so many expenditures in today's world that you would end up without any savings if you don't plan and budget your money; the inflows and the outflows. Wealthy people know where their money comes from and where it goes.

An Excel sheet can really help you in this regard.

> *"A budget is telling your money where to go, instead of wondering where it went."- John C. Maxwell*

Action Point Seven: Work hard - Unlike the common perception that wealthy people just have fun and enjoy their life, the reality is that they work harder than the common person. It's important to point out that hard work doesn't mean exhausting yourself trying to push a rock up a hill for someone else. Find your purpose in life and throw every ounce of your passion, energy and love into it. Most millionaires are not sitting on their yacht for ten months of the year. They are workaholics but for them work is not a bind; it is their passion… they would do it forever if they could. If you don't currently feel like that about what you are doing to earn money, I am afraid to say you will never become rich this way.

> *"I like business and the truth is I save way more than I spend. I invest. I plan for the future. I have a special eye for opportunities and work harder than anyone might expect." – Sofia Vergara*

Action Point Eight: Have multiple streams of income: Self-made millionaires do not rely on only a single source of income. Instead, they develop multiple streams, and most have at least three.

"Sixty-five percent had three or more streams of income that they created over time,"

"Diversifying your sources of income allows you to weather the economic downturns that always occur in life."

Revenue streams include real estate rentals, stock market investments, annuities, private equity investments, part ownership in side businesses, ancillary products, or services, and royalties.

"Do not save what is left after spending, but spend what is left after saving." – Warren Buffet

Action Point Nine: The Rules of Cats & Dogs – I want you to think about money a little differently. Imagine for me that poverty is a dog and wealth is a cat. Dogs are very loyal animals they will stay with you through thick and thin. If you want attention from the dog, just focus your time and effort in it's direction and it will reward you with its dedication and affection. This all sounds very lovely but remember in this metaphor the dog is bringing you nothing but poverty and the more you focus on the dog the more dog you get.

What happens when you want attention from a cat? If you grab the cat and try to stroke it, then it will most likely strike at you and run away. If you go running after the cat it will run up a tree out of your reach or scurry under the sofa where you cannot find it. If you are a cat owner you will know first hand they care very little about what you want out of the deal. If you want the attention and affection of the cat you must almost appear to ignore it. While you are busy trying to get on with other stuff the cat will seek out your time and attention. I know from personal experience that the time my cats want me the most is when I am busy at my computer typing away. I normally sit writing with one on my knee and another attempting to lie down on the keyboard. However, one night when I had received some bad news and I was feeling very low I picked up Mishu (our oldest and biggest cat) and tried to give him a hug – he nearly took my face off!

The point of the Rule of Dogs & Cats is this. Wealth is not something you get by going after it. You become rich while you are busy doing something else. Wealth is not measured by how much you want money but rather by how many other people you are helping, how many needs you are fulfilling. If you don't have as much abundance in your life as you want, you must first ask yourself 'how can I serve the needs of people more'? Getting obsessed with money and focusing on it's accumulation will only get you ignored by the very thing you need the most.

Action Point Ten: Don't become a stagnant pond – If you act like Scrooge McDuck and keep all your money hoarded away then despite having wealth you will never reach your full potential. Hoarding money is not very different from being poor. In both circumstances the mindset about money is one of scarcity. This reciprocal law applies to everything in life. If you want more love you can't hope to achieve this end by never giving away your own love to someone else. If you want more money, then make space for money to flow into your life. It might seem counter intuitive to give away money in order to get more money but this is exactly why most people don't ever escape the 80%.

There is an old Chinese proverb that demonstrates this principle well. Once, a long time ago, there was a wise Zen master. People from far and near would seek his counsel and ask for his wisdom. Many would come and ask him to teach them, enlighten them in the way of Zen. He seldom turned any away.

One day an important man, a man used to command and obedience came to visit the master. "I have come today to ask you to teach me about Zen. Open my mind to enlightenment. But before you start I must tell you, I am very successful and have already achieved a lot with my life. So, please skip the basics and get right to the advanced level stuff." The tone of the important man's voice was one used to getting his own way.

The Zen master smiled and said that they should discuss the matter over a cup of tea. When the tea was served the master poured his visitor a cup. He poured and he poured and the tea rose to the rim and began to spill over the table and finally onto the robes of the wealthy man. Finally, the visitor shouted, "Enough. You are spilling the tea all over. Can't you see the cup is full?"

The master stopped pouring and smiled at his guest. "You are like this tea cup, so full that nothing more can be added. Come back to me when the cup is empty. Come back to me with an empty mind."

Essentially when you see money as a fluid element in your life then you create the mindset to allow it to flow in abundance. Ideally you would save a third of your income, give away a third and live on the remaining third. In the real world it will never be as fixed as this but if you are serious about joining the super-rich then give generously to worthy causes and dedicate yourself to helping other people. Remember that classic saying coined by the late, great Zig Ziglar "You will get anything and everything you want in life. If you will just help enough other people to get what they want".

Time is an illusion that you don't control.

"The world is full of abundance and opportunity, but far too many people come to the fountain of life with a sieve instead of a tank car... a teaspoon instead of a steam shovel. They expect little and as a result they get little",
Ben Sweetland

Time, as we know it, is only an illusion. We usually think of time as having three parts - Past, Present, Future. But what is the Past - only a collection of memories. We can't experience the Past, we can only remember it. And we can only remember it in the Present (furthermore, our memories are noticeably unreliable). There is no objective thing that we call the Past; it can't be measured in any way; our only contact with it is in the Present.
And what is the Future - only a mental construct in the Present. We can't experience the Future until it "becomes" the Present. Until then it only a hope and dream. We can project what the Future may be like, but we are considerably less accurate than when we remember the Past. There is no objective thing that we call the Future; it can't be measured in any way; our only contact with it is in the Present.
That leaves us with only the Present - the ever changing Present. Actually if you want to true to yourself about time you should wear a watch that simply says 'now', but you may pretty quickly establish a reputation for being late.

It's actually the impatience of the ego that creates the compelling arguments that our prayers are not answered. If you subconsciously believe in something, it will happen, that much is automatic and there is nothing that can stop it happening. The frustration for us to accept is that we don't really know when is best for that thing to arrive. However, the universe absolutely does and your dream will be delivered at the precise moment when it is best for you to experience it. Your prayer is answered in the perfect moment it was always intended to be, not a second before or after that point.

What we must accept is that to flow like the river we must arrive at the sea when the river dictates and not when we believe we should be there. The Millionaire Mindset is as similar to the genie in the lamp story as it is poles apart from it. You really can manifest anything and everything you desire but it is not as simple as rubbing a dirty lamp and finding your dreams appear before you in a flash of light and a puff of white smoke. So before you start dreaming and praying for all the things you believe you need to be happy ask yourself the question 'is everything not perfect just as it is'. There is an old saying that goes 'be careful what you wish for' and let me tell you why that is very true.

Many years ago I dreamed that my words would reach thousands of people just like you. I thought the principles I was starting to live my life by could help many, many other people around the world given the chance to hear them. As a slight aside to the point I will tell you that I am probably most proud of my work on alcohol addiction because I believe there are millions of hard working people drinking a bottle of wine a night under the illusion that they are normal (because its also what their friends do) and they are not addicted to a powerful and deceptive drug. I struggled with alcohol for nearly seventeen years until I changed the way I subconsciously felt about the act of drinking and then as if by magic one day I just stopped and for good, I did it without pain or will power.

Despite having tried to quit many times before this time I just knew I would never drink again. That is how you can tell the switch has been flicked in the opposite direction. When you don't just 'think it' but you actually 'know it', at that point you don't have to fight or swim furiously up the stream. Suddenly the water appears to be flowing exactly to where you want to go and you can relax and float along with the current, what you desire will just appear exactly as the water will always reach the ocean. I don't ever crave a drink and even in the middle of a party where everyone is chugging back the booze the last thing I was to do is join them.

I promise I am heading back to the point I was about the make but If you are interested to know more about my method to stop drinking then I strongly urge you to download my audiobook ' Alcohol Lied To Me' or visit www.stopdrinkingexpert.com

'Be careful what you wish for' they say, and with good reason. I didn't just think I wanted my work to be published and released to the world I knew it was going to happen. There was never a fragment of doubt in my mind, body or soul. I flicked the switch and passed a command to the universe, it was going to be delivered to me no matter what happened. Obviously my ego insisted that it arrived immediately if not sooner. I was sure I was ready and I enthusiastically sent my first two books to dozens of carefully researched publishers.

Over the following six months a slow tide of rejection letters landed in my mailbox. I didn't expect it to be a walk in the park and so I prepared the manuscripts for my second book and sent another giant batch of proposals. Again another half a year passed and my mailbox again filled with polite rejections. I had such unshakable faith in what I was writing I was absolutely dumbstruck by the lack of interest.

I was just about the start on my third blitz to the publishing houses when my life hit a major roadblock. Even as I sit here now I am struggling to think of the words to sum up how bad my life became for a period of nine months. It felt like my whole world came crashing down around me, everything and I really do mean everything that could go wrong did exactly that.

It started with my company losing its main contract with a radio station in the North East of England. This probably accounted for 75% of my income and it was gone over the course of a disastrous meeting one Friday morning at the company HQ. Next, my son started to have a problem with bullying at his school and as a result was coming home in tears virtually every day. As I tried to reassure him in the midst of a financial disaster that I had to deal with urgently, cracks in my marriage started to appear and while I didn't know it at the time, we had started on the unstoppable journey toward separation and divorce.

I would dearly love to report that was the end of our misfortune for that year. One by one another plate that had been previously spinning perfectly started to wobble and fall off. All my investments crashed and became less than worthless overnight. I went from being relatively well off to being close to bankrupt in the space of three months. I had borrowed heavily to create a property portfolio and one at a time I watch each one lose more and more value every month until I got to the point where I owed nearly a million dollars and if I sold everything I owned I would still owe nearly half that amount.

I eventually managed to replace the missing income but it would mean I would be away from home 80% of my life. I would need to travel around the world to replace what I had previously got from one local location. This new situation brought to marriage to it's knees and I found myself waking up feeling like I was a failure who had let his children down, had no option but to declare bankruptcy and was on a direct track to the divorce courts.

For the next three months I awoke each morning and thought 'what's the point' and 'why carry on'. What I forgot is that even the most dramatic of thunderstorm comes to and end. There has never been an earthquake that has lasted forever. What we know Lao Tzu was trying to tell us 2500 years ago is that everything is temporary and hidden within the dark clouds is the clear sky waiting to break through.

Only when I reached the point where I could no longer summon the energy to continue swimming up the river and gave in. Finally accepting that even in the worst case scenario everything would still be just perfect then things started to change. What I mean by that is that I reached an acceptance that the river is going to come down the mountain whether I wanted it to or not. If I had to lose everything I had ever worked to attain, if I had to go bankrupt and if my marriage failed then it was okay. I figured I would still have what is in my head, I would still be who I am as a person, my wonderful children would still call me dad and I would still be free to start all over again on another exciting a fantastic journey.

Early in this book you read about discovering the freedom of dying before your death. To disconnect yourself from everything that you can't take with you when you die. I didn't realize it at the time but this is what I managed to achieve, I found myself in a place where none of the material possessions I had previously cared about really seemed to matter anymore. My accountant tried to drum into me how serious my situation was and he sat there completely bemused by how lightly I appeared to be taking his words. I had already accepted that it would all go, it would all be taken away from me and suddenly it stopped hurting.

As the people I really care about in my life continued to run around with their arms in the air declaring the end of the world is nigh I calmly sat down at my computer and began to rewrite my first two books. The Fragment of God and Swallow The Happy Pill.

Today I have over twenty published books; the New Science Of Persuasion & Influence topped the UK business books chart in 2011. 'The Hypnotic Salesman' was the number one business book in the US, UK and Australia this year and made it to number four on the top one hundred audiobooks sold in the world! Thousands of people have stopped drinking because of 'Alcohol Lied To Me' and my inbox is never empty as a result of all the amazing people who I get to interact with on a daily basis as a result of my work.

Here is the point of the rags to riches story... only the universe knows what needs to happen in order for your dreams to become reality. That is why I tell you to be careful what you wish for. There is no way on earth I would have chosen the path I have been on. However, I am immensely grateful for it because I am only who I am now because of that entire trauma I went through during that dark period in my life. The massive pain I experienced in my every waking moment changed me so profoundly that it forced me to approach everything differently. I rewrote the books and I submitted them to just one publisher, the rest they say is history.

So as we sit in the middle of one of life's storms wondering why our prayers are being ignored, be assured that the storm is actually the byproduct of your prayers being answered and in that moment you are sitting on the workbench of God, being crafted and chiseled into the person you long to be. The pain you experience in the dark times is the same pain the carbon feels as it is squeezed and compressed into a beautiful diamond.

The most stunning, precious stones have all been polished into perfection by the harshest and most violent storms nature can throw at them. You are no different, and so I encourage you to stop trying to accelerate time in the bad times and slow it down in the good. Embrace the hard periods of life because they simply mean great things are on the way. Remember people don't ride rollercoasters for the slow trundle up the inclines, they accept the tedious journey up to enjoy the thrilling ride down.

Be the Dream

"You don't have to be a genius or a visionary or even a college graduate to be successful. You just need a framework and a dream", Michael Dell

Do you remember back at the start of the book when I said that the people who voted for Trump in the United States and Brexit in the United Kingdom are unlikely to see any dramatic change in their situation? That opening chapter was based on a blog post I wrote hours after it was revealed the famous blue walls had collapsed and Hilary Clinton had conceded to her opponent. I am a British guy who lives in Europe, I endorsed neither Clinton nor Trump, I am nothing more than an observer. While a lot of people agreed and commented positively there were a handful of people who were very angry at the piece I had written and me in general. They made statements like 'it might be true for people like you who have a privileged background' and 'how would a rich guy have any idea what the working man feels like'.

The major problem with these objections is they assume I come from a different planet, the planet 'Rich Guy'. They assume that it can't possibly be true that anyone could become successful and wealthy, unless they inherited or scammed their fortune out of the poor unfortunate workingman. Let's be clear, my father was a butcher in the North East of England and the rest of my family were predominantly steel workers. I come from a pure working class background. The problem with people, who are trapped in the 80%, is that they can't accept that the person responsible for their misery might just be themselves and themselves alone! They prefer to be a victim because this gets them attention.

There is nothing wrong with attention; we learn how to crave it from the moment we are born. We cry and our mother comes along to soothe us. Craving love and affection is not only normal but it is essential. Back in the day there was a pretty cruel experiment carried out on Russian orphans. Twenty newborn infants were housed in a special facility. They had caregivers who would go in to feed them, bathe them and change their diapers, but they would do nothing else. The caregivers had been instructed not to look at or touch the babies more than was necessary, and they never spoke to them. All their physical needs were attended to scrupulously, however. The environment was kept sterile; the babies were never ill.

The experiment was halted after four months. At least half of the babies had died at that point, at least two more died even after being rescued and brought into a more normal environment. There was no physiological cause for the babies' deaths; they were all physically very healthy. Before each baby died, there was a period where they would stop crying completely and stop trying to engage their caregivers. They would just stop moving, never make a sound or change expression. Death would follow shortly. The babies who had "given up" before being rescued died in the same manner, even though they had been removed from the experimental conditions.

But there is a huge difference between affection and attention. Being a victim gets you attention but it does not get you affection, nobody really loves being around a victim. You will also find it virtually impossible to find a victim millionaire. If you play the blame game and delegate responsibility for your life to other people you will never be rich. The two states are complete contradictory states of existence.

So if you want to be poor then be a poor victim. But if you want to reach your full potential then quit blaming and be the outcome you desire, it really is as simple as that. Want to be wealthy? Then act wealthy, be grateful for the wealth that you have, even if you have nothing but a few coins in your pocket be grateful for them. Instead of thinking about yesterday when you had more coins or predicting that by tomorrow you will have none at all. Stay in the moment of now and love the fact that you have money.

Act like you have money, I don't mean go waste it on desires of your ego but give it away if the Primary Thought Events tells you that's what you should do. When you give away something the subconscious assumes you must have plenty and so it works to create that reality. Who would have thought that giving away money creates more money? Hey and you know what, it works with everything; want more love? Then give more love! But remember that (free will) safety switch is always turned off, give away abuse and negativity and guess what your life gets more of?

By the way there is nothing wrong with wanting more money as long as you always remember that money is just an idea and nothing more. What we believe money to be is actually nothing of the sort. The currency in our pocket is nothing more that an I.O.U, the money in your bank account is nothing more than numbers on a screen. Because money is a made up concept you can have as much as you imagine you should have.

Some say that money makes the world go round, whilst that's not strictly true and the world would continue quite happily without the concept of money. Cash does flow and circulate like blood coursing around a body and if you stop that natural momentum of wealth by hoarding what you have, by acting like Scrooge you prevent more of what you crave flowing into your life. It sounds illogical at first but in reality the giving of money creates a multi level subconscious portal to open. The amount you give away (without expecting anything back in return) is relative to the size of hole it creates in your person attraction field. Money pours in through this vortex, like water surging through a plughole.

The secondary level benefit of this proven law of The Millionaire Mindset is subliminal damage to what Stephen Covey calls the scarcity mindset. Your subconscious cannot tell the difference between reality and a vividly imagined event. So whether you are wealthy or just believe you are wealthy it's all the same thing at an unconscious level. Logically, therefore if you are freely giving away money to worthy causes that have touched your heart or inspired you somehow then you simply cannot be afraid to lose money and money cannot be a scarce resource.

Most people who attempt a will power based diet will at some point stall in their progress as their subconscious protection systems become aware that food appears to be in limited supply. The body switches to starvation mode to hang on to the very thing you want to lose, that big wobbly belly! The exact same principle applies to your finances, if your mind switches into scarcity mode for anything you can be assured you will get nothing but everything you don't want. Scarcity mode prevents the flow of money by attempting to damn the river and stockpile what you have. This prevents the flow of money from entering your life.

Of course there is a danger hidden within the words of this book. What I write here with good intentions to encourage you to find peace can just as easily be interpreted by your ego as an excuse to ride rough shot over other people's feelings on a new 'permitted' journey to find pleasure. So far I have told you that the rules of other people create misery, bad and good don't really exist and you should let go and forgive yourself of your past mistakes. In the egoic mind of an unawakened soul this could appear to be a license to do pretty much anything you feel like doing, regardless of the impact it has on others.

The easily made error is to confuse pleasure with happiness. Happiness comes from within not from without and does not require any external element to be present. Pleasure is only the shadow that happiness casts against the wall. Pleasure is so shallow that it can be generated purely from the respite from misery. If you were chained to the wall in a foreign jail cell and cruel prison guards tortured you for hours on end. When they stopped whilst you would still be in pain the level will have dropped and it's this improvement that many people assume is happiness.

If you are 100% unhappy with your life because you are overweight, in a job you hate, poor and lonely. Then the situation is changed by some good fortune and you win a small amount on the lottery, which pays off a few bills but not enough to allow you to quit your job. Your level of measured unhappiness is now 80%. By experiencing the drop from 100 to 80 you assume you have discovered happiness, the money made you happy right? Wrong you are still 80% unhappy.

On the 12th July 1964 Nelson Mandela stood before a judge and jury charged with an array of politically motivated crimes against the state. He summed up his defense by saying "During my lifetime I have dedicated myself to the struggle of the African people. I have fought against white domination, and I have fought against black domination. I have cherished the ideal of a democratic and free society in which all persons live together in harmony and with equal opportunities. It is an ideal which

I hope to live for and to achieve. But if needs be, it is an ideal for which I am prepared to die".

With that moving statement he was promptly sentenced to life imprisonment and spent the next 27 years locked in a tiny cell on his own.

Meet Nelson Mandela today and he is one of the most optimistic, smiling, contented and happy of men you will ever meet. How? Mandela was dealt a hand so much more severe and unfair than the one most of us got. After nearly three decades in solitary confinement how is he not a broken shell of a man?

Nelson Mandela understood that people can persecute you, hurt you and cage you away from the light of day but they can never extinguish the perfect flame that burns within you. To keep that flame alive all you must do is be aware of it.

Happiness is within and pleasure is always without. The delusion of the ego is that it incorrectly believes it can take pleasure and convert it into happiness. This is like trying to make an omelet out of a photographs of some eggs. It appears you have the right ingredients but pleasure is just no more real than the reflection of yourself in the mirror is real.

A luxurious piece of chocolate cake with butter cream icing tastes amazing at first and gives you intense pleasure but what happens if you follow your ego and try to make that pleasure permanent by continuing to eat slice after slice of that rich cake. All you have done is repeat the thing that created pleasure but now you feel the opposite, you feel sick and uncomfortable. Suddenly the thing you believed was pleasurable now doesn't taste very good at all.

A clear indicator of when you are obeying the commands of your ego is when you pursue more of something. Your ego can never be satisfied and will always demand more of everything it believes will generate pleasure.

When you open a bottle of fine wine and take that first sip allowing the rich and flavorsome liquid to tingle over your pallet and swamp your taste buds with its intoxicating taste. Why don't you put the bottle away having experienced the pleasure you initially craved, why is it necessary to pour a second glass? Is it not true that the second glass doesn't quite taste as good as the first? And how good does the tenth glass of that wine taste?

Pleasure is the shadow cast on the wall by happiness but no matter how many shadow puppets you make at no point will they become real. Trying to make pleasure permanent is like filling a leaking barrel of water with a bucket. You will spend a lifetime not quite getting anywhere.

Whenever you want more of something it is nothing but your ego making a demand and this applies to everything. If you believe that more money will make you happy you are being lied to by yourself. If you think more love is all you need to feel content you will find that there is simply not enough love in the world to ever satisfy you. Even if you believe that all that is wrong with your life is you need more sex and passion you will find that there is never quite enough to tick the box.

This does not mean you shouldn't partake in pleasurable things, you should do what you feel you need to do but be aware you are satisfying needs of the ego and nothing more. Your thinking mind can be distracted and amused with the most simple and basic of acts. I am almost certain you have laughed at the sight of someone else falling over in the past, is another persons accident really pleasurable or is it the ego's delight that the misfortune didn't happen to you the real source of the amusement.

The German's even have a name for this black humor. 'Schadenfreude' is defined as pleasure derived from the misfortunes of others. Surely we have all at some point taken pleasure from the misfortune of others.

When I worked as a late night radio presenter for a commercial radio station in the North West of the United Kingdom I would have to prepare for my nightly broadcast in a shared open plan office. Another local radio station in our company had their studios in the same building. One Monday night the usual guy didn't show up and instead a new presenter called Tony who had been given the competing show to mine on our sister station walked through the door. I greeted him and showed him where the coffee machine was located, almost as essential as oxygen to us late night guys.

As I showed him around and made polite small talk he stopped and looked me straight in the eye and snarled 'I am going to wipe the floor with you'. I was quite taken aback; I had never considered the other station a threat to me as we were both focusing on completely different audience demographics. I was on a young contemporary hit music station and he was on an AM talk format.

"You are going to regret the day I walked into this place, I am coming after all your audience and when I am finished with you there will be no doubt as to who is cutting it at this time of day in this patch", he continued with some seriously unnecessary venom in his words.

Our relationship never really got any better than that and far from cause me a problem he continued to struggle in the ratings for nearly eighteen month. Until the station he worked for approached me and asked me to come over to their side not only as a broadcaster but also as the manager of the station. My brief was to improve the audience figures and it was very clear who was first to go in the big overhaul of the brand.

I called Tony in and as professionally and politely as I could I informed him that we were not renewing his contract and parting company. He broke down in tears, emptied his locker into a plastic bag and headed for the door. Did it upset me firing Tony? No not really in fact I will admit a little dark side of me thought it couldn't have happened to a nicer guy and I was almost glad it was my finger on the trigger. But did it make me happy? No.

Pleasure is part of why we choose to experience life in physical form but to be happy you should be able to strip away all pleasure and still feel content. Pleasure is sedation for the ego and having a human ego is similar to carrying around with you a priceless crystal glass. You can show the glass off and revel in the attention that it brings, you can fill the glass with fine wine but the price you pay for carrying this delicate and precious article around with you is it can be very easily damaged or smashed by others. Happiness is different because it resides protected within, enveloped by your soul and untouchable by anyone but you.

And now as a special treat for your subconscious mind only, I will tell you the story of the two travellers:

One day a traveler was walking along a road on his journey from one village to another. As he walked he noticed a monk tilling the ground in the fields beside the road. The monk said "Good day" to the traveler and the traveler nodded to the monk. The traveler then turned to the monk and said, "Excuse me, do you mind if I ask you a question?"

"Not at all," replied the monk.

"I am traveling from the village in the mountains to the village in the valley and I was wondering if you knew what it is like in the village in the valley?"

"Tell me," said the monk. "What was your experience of the village in the mountains?"

"Dreadful," replied the traveler. "To be honest I am glad to be away from there. I found the people most unwelcoming. When I first arrived I was greeted coldly. I was never made to feel a part of the village no matter how hard I tried. The villagers keep very much to themselves; they don't take kindly to strangers. So tell me, what can I expect in the village in the valley?"

"I'm sorry to tell you," said the monk, "but I think your experience will be much the same there."

The traveler hung his head despondently and walked on. A few months later another traveler was journeying down the same road and he also came upon the monk. "Good day," said the traveler.

"Good day," said the monk.

"How are you?" asked the traveler.

"I'm well," replied the monk. "Where are you going?"

"I'm going to the village in the valley," replied the traveler. "Do you know what it is like?"

"I do," replied the monk. "But first, tell me, where have you come from?"

"I've come from the village in the mountains."

"And how was that?"

"It was a wonderful experience. I would have stayed if I could but I am committed to traveling on. I felt as though I were a member of the family in the village. The elders gave me much advice, the children laughed and joked with me, and the people generally were kind and generous. I am sad to have left there. It will always hold special memories for me. And what of the village in the valley?" he asked again.

"I think you will find it much the same," replied the monk. "Good day to you."

"Good day and thank you," replied the traveler, smiled, and journeyed on.

Be the River

"When I think about creating abundance, it's not about creating a life of luxury for everybody on this planet; it's about creating a life of possibility. It is about taking that which was scarce and making it abundant", Peter Diamandis

We live in a temporary reality, nothing can ever be permanent and you are free to waste an entire lifetime finding that out for yourself. Animals know this better than us and is why you never seen animals building permanent structures, homes to live in all their life. Animals don't ever try and own things, they understand that all they have in the current moment is all that matters. The food they had yesterday has gone and trying to predict how much they will have tomorrow is a pointless activity.

As I sit writing this chapter of The Millionaire Mindset a formation of geese have just flown overhead in a perfect and silent V shaped flight pattern. Whilst the goose at the head of the V has to work considerably harder than the others he doesn't complain or resent the other members of the group. Instinctively when he tires another goose will silently move into position and allow the tiring animal to move into the less resistant slipstream. If geese had a human ego then they would fall from the sky in a shambolic and violent argument as the lead goose declared how unfair it is that he must shoulder the burden of the increased wind resistance at the front of the V.

Animals are less cursed by the negative effects of the ego and simply flow in the stream of nature. They never try to make themselves more attractive, when was the last time you saw a rabbit styling its hair? Animals just exist in the temporary perfection of life and there is a profound lesson waiting for you by pausing in the middle of the chaos of your life and observing animals and insects.

Watch a spider build it's web, be aware of how in the moment it lives. The spider creates an amazing and intricate construction. Swat away the web and does the spider down tools in temper, throw the towel in and give up or does it simply start again? Does the spider ever demonstrate anger that you ruined all its hard work, or does it work slower on the second web because it is disappointed to have to repeat the task over again?

No the spider doesn't care about what went before, it is gone and as only the ego lives in the past and a spider doesn't have an ego it is of no concern. Neither are concerns of whether that web will still be there tomorrow, without the curse of the ego (the precise thing we in the western world believe makes us superior) nothing exists but the precise moment.

Humans on the other hand are driven by their crazy egos that demand that we find more and more ways to avoid the inevitable. We are always trying to build our perceived levels of significance by trying to own more and more things. We buy cars, houses, art and other trappings that we can point to and say look how important I am. The futility of this will become more and more apparent to you the older you get. I know multi millionaires who are now in what we would describe as the twilight of their lives who would gladly give away every single penny for the chance to be young again. I equally know as many young people who would give up everything for the chance to be rich – youth really is wasted on the young!

One of the best pieces of advice I ever heard is to remember that life is just a piece of theatre and you are one of its actors. Your life and everything in it is just your part in the script. It is not who you really are and the bad things are not really happening it's all an illusion the secret is to strip away the ego that believe you are the character you are playing and see that you are instead the actor enjoying his work hidden beneath the greasepaint and make up.

If you are struggling to see how you can live like a creature devoid of an ego when you are clearly a human being suffering with that very affliction I can tell you that for most people there is a point in your life when you will be able to experience that exact state of being. Sadly when you reach this point you are normally months, weeks or days away from death. When people are diagnosed with terminal illness and after they have allowed the conscious mind to fruitlessly try to push the river back up the stream. When they reach the point where they stop swimming against the stream and let go, they accept the inevitable a profound and beautiful peace wraps itself around them.

In this moment when they have accepted and stopped fighting against death the ego begins to die. In the final days these people experience awareness of life from a purely divine prospective for the first and last time in their life they see the truth.

Bronnie Ware is a palliative care nurse who for many years worked purely with people who had been sent home to die. The medical profession could do no more for them and the only remaining objective was to ensure a pain free death in a comfortable and familiar environment. As Bronnie helped these people and got to know them over their final weeks she started to notice that there were some very common threads amongst the things they said of their lives on earth.

Bronnie started to make notes on what these dying people were saying and she realized that there were five main observations that were made by virtually all people who knew they were about to past away.

1. I wish I'd had the courage to live a life true to myself, not the life others expected of me.
This was the most common regret of all. When people realize that their life is almost over and look back clearly on it, it is easy to see how many dreams have gone unfulfilled. Most people have had not honored even a half

of their dreams and had to die knowing that it was due to choices they had made, or not made.
It is very important to try and honor at least some of your dreams along the way. From the moment that you lose your health, it is too late. Health brings a freedom very few realize, until they no longer have it.

2. I wish I didn't work so hard.
This came from every male patient that Bronnie nursed. They missed their children's youth and their partner's companionship. Women also spoke of this regret. But as most were from an older generation, many of the female patients had not been breadwinners. All of the men she nursed deeply regretted spending so much of their lives on the treadmill of a work existence.
By simplifying your lifestyle and making conscious choices along the way, it is possible to not need the income that you think you do. And by creating more space in your life, you become happier and more open to new opportunities, ones more suited to your new lifestyle.

3. I wish I'd had the courage to express my feelings.
Many people suppressed their feelings in order to keep peace with others. As a result, they settled for a mediocre existence and never became who they were truly capable of becoming. Many developed illnesses relating to the bitterness and resentment they carried as a result.
We cannot control the reactions of others. However, although people may initially react when you change the way you are by speaking honestly, in the end it raises the relationship to a whole new and healthier level. Either

that or it releases the unhealthy relationship from your life. Either way, you win.

4. I wish I had stayed in touch with my friends.
Often they would not truly realize the full benefits of old friends until their dying weeks and it was not always possible to track them down. Many had become so caught up in their own lives that they had let golden friendships slip by over the years. There were many deep regrets about not giving friendships the time and effort that they deserved. Everyone misses their friends when they are dying.

It is common for anyone in a busy lifestyle to let friendships slip. But when you are faced with your approaching death, the physical details of life fall away. People do want to get their financial affairs in order if possible. But it is not money or status that holds the true importance for them. They want to get things in order more for the benefit of those they love. Usually though, they are too ill and weary to ever manage this task. Despite what your ego believe now it all comes down to love and relationships in the end. That is all that remains in the final weeks, love and relationships.

5. I wish that I had let myself be happier.
This is a surprisingly common one. Many did not realize until the end that happiness is a choice. They had stayed stuck in old patterns and habits. The so-called 'comfort' of familiarity overflowed into their emotions, as well as their physical lives. Fear of change had them pretending to others, and to their selves, that they were content. When

deep within, they longed to laugh properly and have silliness in their life again.

You can choose to continue pushing the river up the hill and wait for this knowing to finally arrive into your life, granted at a point where you can't do anything with the knowledge but pass it on to others. Or you can decide to change your life today, to stop kicking and allow the water to carry you to where it wants to take you.

While you allow that message to permeate your subconscious mind, I will close this chapter with the story of the carrot, the egg, and the coffee bean

A young woman went to her mother and told her about her life and how things were so hard for her. She did not know how she was going to make it and wanted to give up. She was tired of fighting and struggling.

It seemed that, as one problem was solved, a new one arose. Her mother took her to the kitchen. She filled three pots with water and placed each on a high fire. Soon the pots came to a boil. In the first, she placed carrots, in the second she placed eggs, and in the last she placed ground coffee beans.

She let them sit and boil, without saying a word. In about twenty minutes, she turned off the burners. She fished the carrots out and placed them in a bowl. She pulled the eggs out and placed them in a bowl. Then she ladled the coffee out and placed it in a bowl. Turning to her daughter, she asked, "Tell me, what do you see?"

"Carrots, eggs, and coffee," the young woman replied. The mother brought her closer and asked her to feel the carrots. She did and noted that they were soft. She then asked her to take an egg and break it. After pulling off the shell, she observed the hard-boiled egg. Finally, she asked her to sip the coffee. The daughter smiled as she tasted its rich aroma. The daughter then asked, "What does it mean, mother?"

Her mother explained that each of these objects had faced the same adversity - boiling water - but each reacted differently. The carrot went in strong, hard and unrelenting. However, after being subjected to the boiling water, it softened and became weak.

The egg had been fragile. Its thin outer shell had protected its liquid interior. But, after sitting through the boiling water, its inside became hardened! The ground coffee beans were unique, however. After they were in the boiling water, they had changed the water.

"Which are you?" the mother asked her daughter. "When adversity knocks on your door, how do you respond? Are you a carrot, an egg, or a coffee bean?" Think of this: Which am I? Am I the carrot that seems strong but, with pain and adversity, do I wilt and become soft and lose my strength? Am I the egg that starts with a malleable heart, but changes with the heat? Did I have a fluid spirit but, after a death, a breakup, or a financial hardship, does my shell look the same, but on the inside am I bitter and tough with a stiff spirit and a hardened heart? Or am I like the coffee bean? The bean actually changes the hot water, the very circumstance that brings the pain. When the water gets hot, it releases the fragrance and flavor.

If you are like the bean, when things are at their worst, you get better and change the situation around you. When the hours are the darkest and trials are their greatest, do you elevate to another level? How do you handle adversity? Are you a carrot, an egg, or a coffee bean?

V is for Victim

"Let me tell you something you already know. The world ain't all sunshine and rainbows. It's a very mean and nasty place, and I don't care how tough you are, it will beat you to your knees and keep you there permanently if you let it. You, me, or nobody is gonna hit as hard as life.

But it ain't about how hard you hit. It's about how hard you can get hit and keep moving forward; how much you can take and keep moving forward. That's how winning is done! Now, if you know what you're worth, then go out and get what you're worth. But you gotta be willing to take the hits, and not pointing fingers saying you ain't where you wanna be because of him, or her, or anybody. Cowards do that and that ain't you. You're better than that!

I'm always gonna love you, no matter what. No matter what happens. You're my son and you're my blood. You're the best thing in my life. But until you start believing in yourself, you ain't gonna have a life", Rocky Balboa

I want to tell you about Katie, I am sure you know her already, perhaps not the same Katie but certainly 'a Katie'. Poor Katie drew a bad hand in life; she didn't do great at school because as she tells the story the teachers were idiots. She always dreamed of a cool apartment overlooking the sea, with a little dog called

Jack. Unfortunately because her boss is an asshole she has to rent a crumby flat in a rough part of town and due to the fact the Mr. Brown the landlord is a total douche and doesn't allow pets she is not allowed to get a dog.

Talk to Katie yourself and she will tell you how unfair life is and how she deserves so much more than such and such a person and yet they have everything she wants. She will tell you that nobody really understands her and all her friends are two-faced bitches who are out to cause as much trouble as possible.

Is it possible that Katie just got an unlucky break in life, is there any chance that she is correct in her assessment of life? Let's put it this way, there is more chance of Donald Trump denouncing racism and promoting love and peace for all men than Katie being accurate in her assessment of why she is not living the life she wants. Katie is a victim and these victims are everywhere – we can't move for them. These are the people that believe life owes them something and they often spend an entire lifetime furious that the neighbor got yet another new car or so and so got promoted at work when they are quite clearly incompetent.

Victims not only suck the energy out of their own lives but anyone who comes close enough to get caught up in their vortex of doom. They are mood hoovers and I am almost certain you can think of at least a few people who fit perfectly into this description. Let's first talk about how you deal with this trait in other people and then I want you to have a little honesty session about areas of your life where you have adopted the roll of victim, because its easier than facing the hard truth.

How do you help a victim? The short answer is you can't, because they don't want to be helped. They like being the victim; it gives them a convenient explanation as to why their life blows chunks. On their deathbed you could ask them 'why didn't you live the life you were truly capable of' and they will have enough plausible deniability to stubbornly point at something or someone and say 'because of that'. All the time they are pointing a finger of blame at everything and everyone around them they are blissfully unaware they have three fingers pointed right back at them. It is really frustrating to care about a victim because you can see the huge untapped potential in them but they cannot. When they look in the mirror all they see is someone who has been badly treated by life.

If they are a family member, or even perhaps your son or daughter you will desperately try to help them see the truth but in my experience all you will end up doing is expending vast amounts of energy to get precisely nowhere with them. The harsh reality is this; we are all divine creators of life. We each have a fragment of God embedded within us and we all have the power to perform our own miracles. If we take decisive action and flow with the universe instead of kicking violently to go back up stream we can manifest breathtakingly amazing lives for ourselves. Victims have this power too but they choose to ignore it.

How to spot a victim

Victims have reasons, lots of them and often they seem entirely logical and plausible explanations.

- I am ill because the doctor gave me the wrong medicine
- I am poor because my boss is a jerk
- I got fired because I am a woman
- I got made redundant because I am black
- They won't employ me because I am white
- I can't quit drinking because it's the only pleasure I have left.
- I am too stressed to stop smoking

The list goes on and on and all of it is 100% proof bullshit. There are four certainties in this life. You will be born, you will die and in between you will pay tax and life will repeatedly knock you down. As Rocky Balboa says 'Ain't nothing going to hit as hard as life'. Getting knocked down is not bad luck anymore than turning on the tap and getting water could be considered luck. Life is getting knocked down, the choice is getting back up again looking it in the eye and saying 'is that all you got, hit me again but this time put some effort in it you big girl's blouse'.

The reason you can't help the victims is when they get knocked down they love it. It gives them what they want, an excuse not to get back up again. They are like boxers who are too tired to keep fighting hoping for one decent punch so they can fall down with dignity and stay the hell down until the referee counts ten.

Exercise

Stop reading for ten minutes and think about the victims in your life. Ask yourself who they are, how long they have been there and most importantly how much time are you spending trying to make them feel better. Which by the way is like trying to push oil uphill. Once you are clear about who these people are I want you to make a conscious decision to spend less and less time in their company – until they are no longer a part of your life. That's right I am asking you to fire the mood hovers in your life, you can't help them, they are not helping you so it's time for them to leave.

But wait… what if you are the victim?

Are you a victim? This is a pretty easy question to answer; think of something in your life that you are not happy with. For example lets say you need more money. Now with that problem in mind explain to yourself why this is your current situation. If you find you have answers and excuses readily available (such as because my boss keeps overlooking me for promotion) then you are operating in a victim mindset around this area. If your response is more positive and places responsibility on your own shoulders then you are in an abundance mindset (for example – I took a pay cut to change direction in my career but I know if I give this new job 100% I am going to earn ten times the amount I would have in the old role).

Having an abundance mindset always starts with you taking 100% responsibility. Let me give you an example from my own life. In 2007 I bought a villa in Cyprus, I didn't know it at the time but I was investing at possibly the worst time in the last century. Property prices were hugely overinflated and there was a mad rush of eager buyers trying to get in on what was being touted as a gold rush. Realtors were promising anyone who would listen that you could easily double your money within a few short years. I had always wanted to live in the sunshine by the sea so I went all in. Three months after I collected the keys to my property the Lehman Brothers collapsed and the whole western world went into a financial meltdown. Overnight my property lost 40% of its value but that was irrelevant, as the whole market had evaporated. Due to a concrete explosion over the past few years the tiny island of Cyprus found itself with thousands and thousands of new build property and absolutely no buyers to be seen. To make matters worse I had taken a mortgage in Swiss francs on the advice of the bank. Because Switzerland was considered a safe haven outside the crashing dollar, pound and euro their currency value went through the roof. My mortgage payments tripled over night.

Whose fault is this disastrous investment? The victim would say it's the realtor for advising me badly; it's the bank for selling me a volatile product or any other number of villains that could be pointed at and labeled as the 'fault' behind this mess. At the point where you create an excuse you become a reaction to life. You are a passenger who is responding to the events of life that are thrust upon you. Conversely when you accept 100% responsibility for the events around you then you are in the driving seat. Let me tell you, when you are alone in a runaway car the last place you want to be is in the passenger seat.

My thoughts about the house in Cyprus are this: It is my responsibility, I created it and I will solve it. I don't believe it was a mistake, I believe it is a blessing here in my life to push me in a specific direction, to challenge me, to teach me and ultimately to make me stronger. When the time is right the situation will resolve one way or another.

I run a website for men called Powerfully Confident. I help guys build their self-belief and self esteem. One of the most common problems I face time and time again is the victim mindset. Guys will state that they can't find the woman of their dreams because they are too short, not good looking enough, not educated enough, not interesting enough or any other of a million excuses. I always tell them that before we can work together any further they must go and read about a guy called Nick Vujicic.

Nick Vujicic was born without any arms or legs. The closest thing he has to a useable extremity is what should have been his left leg. Looking nothing like a human leg, it is a small protrusion that he affectionately refers to as his chicken drumstick. He uses the limited motion of this appendage to control his electric wheelchair.

Can you imagine what childhood was like for this guy? He grew up always feeling different, always feeling left out. Watching his friends run, jump and play soccer. Always the spectator and never the protagonist. Sure he has had his moments of despair and openly admits that he has been to some dark places but he chooses to do the opposite of what you would expect. Rather than wallow in his misfortune he chooses to embrace the life he has been given. Despite all the odds, he is an exceptionally talented and popular motivational speaker. He tours the world speaking to schoolchildren about positive thinking and self esteem. If you have never heard of this guy I encourage you to get on YouTube and watch some of his videos, if he doesn't move you to tears within a few minutes I insist you get checked for a working heart as soon as possible.

When Nick goes to speak to a group of children they normally watch in stunned silence as he is helped onto a table at the front of the assembly hall. The severely disabled and yet smiling man in front of them mesmerizes the ordinarily raucous group of youngsters. Such is the stillness in the room that you could hear a pin drop. Nick breaks this profound silence by challenging them to a game of soccer and a nervous laugh fills the room. Nick Vujicic is so full of positive loving energy that it causes the whole room to radiate with they most amazing and tangible peace.

By the end of the talk, the dozens of girls who had previously cried themselves to sleep thinking about the words of a bully are now crying in joy and love for the man who found happiness against all odds. Love pours out of every cell in this guy's little body as he sits there propped up on a table and dares to ask the kids if they think he is beautiful. Without a flicker of hesitation or doubt the whole room agrees that he is an amazing and stunningly beautiful person. There is a very real mass awakening as children realize the true gift of their own life. The child who hates her freckles suddenly realizes just how perfect she really is. The boy who is bullied for being overweight suddenly understands his true worth. Each and every child sees their own potential.

But surely when it comes to sex and women Nick has a valid excuse right? No, a few years ago Nick Vujicic married his sweetheart, and let me tell you, she is stunningly beautiful. They now have an amazing, healthy son and if you see pictures of Nick and his wife you will see two of the happiest people you ever saw. The beautiful woman at his side is a reflection of the man inside the body. Nick Vujicic is full of love, he is aware of his limitations but he believes that he is a valuable human being with the ability to enhance the lives of all those around him. But the single most important aspect of Nick's success is he is not a victim. Of course he had the choice to become a victim, many times. But he chose to see the opportunities rather than the obstacles.

If you think Nick is a one off and you still believe you have a valid excuse to defend not having the wealth, abundance, happiness and amazing life that you really desire then I will remind you of the story of W. Mitchell:

In 1971, June 19th, he was 28 years old. He didn't have a care in the world. He was a very good-looking guy. He was driving down the freeway in America on his motorbike and not a care in the world. Something caught his attention to the left in a field and he looked to see what it was. When he turned back to concentrate on the road he realized he was travelling at 80 miles an hour towards the back of a truck. He was only 5 ft. away from the truck.

The only thing he could do to save his life was to slam the bike onto the floor so he would slide under the truck. As he slid under the truck the fuel cap came off the motorbike and covered him in gasoline. The sparks from the motorbike ignited the fuel. He was ablaze. Sixty-five per cent of his body had third-degree burns. His face was nearly burnt off. His fingers were stumps. He was unrecognizable. People would visit him in the emergency ward of the hospital and pass out when they saw him. He was that bad.

He was in a coma for two weeks and when he came round would you have blamed him if he said, I can't go on; life is just not worth living? W. Mitchell chose a different path. He realized after time that he didn't have to accept society's notion that to be happy a person must be healthy and good looking. Mitchell came to see it, as he put it I'm in charge of my own spaceship, my own ups and downs. I can choose to see this as either a setback or a new beginning.

Instead of being overcome by his obvious problems and the pain of the therapy he'd have to go through, Mitchell decided to turn those problems into challenges. He joined two friends and he founded a new wood-burning stove company. A few short years later he helped build Vermont Castings into a multimillion-dollar company. He was a millionaire. If you think that's the happy ending of the story, think again.

In 1975, November, disaster struck again. W. Mitchell was sitting on the runway in his own private jet with three friends in the back. He'd forgotten to check the wings for ice and as you probably know ice can cause disaster for planes. As he attempted to take off the plane crashed. His three passengers got out without a mark on them. W. Mitchell was paralysed from the neck down. Mitchell chose to survive and those negative people went up to him and said, somebody must really hate you up there, how are you going to continue? He said, before all this happened there were 10,000 things I could do. Now there are only 9,000. I could spend my life dwelling on the 1,000 that I lost or I could choose to focus on the 9,000 that are left, and that's what he did.

In 1982 he married his sweetheart and in 1984 he ran for Congress. He went door-to-door campaigning and he used the catchphrase, vote for me and I won't be just another pretty face. Mitchell says that he had two big bumps in his life and he chose not to use them as excuses to quit. To become a success, to become wealthy, concentrate on the positive.

Exercise

Stop reading and grab a pen. I want you to write down everything negative in your life that you believe is there because someone else put it there. Then next to each bullet point I want you to come up with a new positive spin that gives you 100% responsibility for the event. Now wait, lets be clear. There is a huge difference between blame and responsibility. I am not asking you to take the blame for the day you got mugged in broad daylight or the night your car got stolen. Fault and blame are pointless actions of the ego, blaming the mugger for attacking you doesn't undo the act of violence that occurred.

What I want you to do here is accept the situation as being a part of your life. You may not have chosen to have it happen but for whatever reason you attracted it in. It's a part of you and that means you are the only person who can heal it within yourself. Make peace with it and try to give yourself a point of view that does precisely zero finger pointing and has a high expectation that a positive outcome will arrive.

These exercises are very easily skipped and forgotten about but please try to do them because they make a huge difference to the speed at which you can effect positive change in your life.

Inside The Vortex

A few years ago, the city council of Monza, Italy, barred pet owners from keeping goldfish in curved bowls... saying that it is cruel to keep a fish in a bowl with curved sides because, gazing out, the fish would have a distorted view of reality. But how do we know we have the true, undistorted picture of reality", Stephen Hawking

The central core of the Millionaire Mindset is the premise that wealth and abundance is a recipe not an event. The recipe for a chocolate cake means that when followed to the letter you will always end up with a chocolate cake. As long who ever if following the instructions, does so meticulously they can't ever end up with anything but a chocolate cake. Therefore this must also be true of wealth and abundance, if you follow the action plan laid out in this book you will one day become rich, there is nothing else that can happen. Now of course if you lose patience with the baking process and turn off the oven half way through the quality of the cake will suffer.

The single most important lesson you can learn about wealth creation is that it is an internally generated element and not a destination that we may end up at or an external event that is bestowed upon us. This is true of everything in life that we want and don't want. More love, happiness, peace and purpose are already inside us. We don't have to go off in search of these things, but rather we need to learn how to release them from within. To do that let us start with the premise that inside each one of us is a divine particle of source. A perfect morsel of the universe that wants for nothing, needs nothing and desires nothing. This part of you consists of one emotion and one emotion only, love. It is acutely aware that it is eternal and that it is one with everything else. It has no fear of death and knows precisely why you are here and what you need to find your own happiness, peace and purpose on earth. This part of you not only knows what your heart desires but it also knows exactly how to give it to you. It is only reasonable for you to wonder then; why do you still not have the life you want?

The reason you still feel that emptiness inside you is because you are currently blocking all the divine elements from entering your life. It's similar to trying to pour yourself a glass of soda with the bottle cap only half loosened. The soda drips into the glass, but not quickly enough to give you anything worthwhile. In the case of the law of attraction and manifesting the life of your dreams, it is not a bottle cap preventing the outcome you desire but seven universal illusions that stop you from seeing what needs to be done to restore the flow. In this penultimate section of Millionaire Mindset, I am going to remind you what the illusions are and show you how to fine-tune your thinking and behavior to permit this powerful life changing force to rush into your life.

If you are wondering why there are seven universal laws, haven't you noticed that it's always seven? Stephen Covey wrote about the seven habits of highly successful people, there were seven brides for the seven brothers and there are seven dwarfs to keep Snow White company. Human's have a secret love affair with the number seven, it makes us feel safe and secure... but that is a wonder we can explore on another day.

The Seven Illusions:

1. **The illusion of separation**

    This first common blockage is centered on the assumption that what we see happening before our eyes is really as it appears! A belief that we are all entirely self-sufficient individuals with no significant connection to anyone who falls outside the circle of our immediate family and friends. Falling for this illusion is like the branches of a tree believing that they have nothing to do with each other.

    When we strip everything down to its atomic level, there is no difference between any of us. We are not just similar: we are made of the exact same material, the same as every other life form or physical object on earth. We are composed of particles of energy vibrating in an infinite variety of frequencies. You can already see how removing this one blockage from the human condition would effectively render racism, sexism and any other *ism* you can think of impossible in one fell swoop.

This illusion forces us to ignore the divinity within us and listen only to the insane ramblings of the ego. This act pushes our vibrational frequency lower and further away from where we need to be to start attracting the life we really desire.

2. The illusion of God

Religion has made quite a few monumentally flawed assumptions about who, what and where God is. Over many thousands of years, traditional religion has taken certain commonly agreed upon facts and leapt to various spurious postulations. One of which is that God is perfect and therefore we are all a pale reflection of his majesty. A species he created from dirt and is a constant sinful disappointment to him (for God is a man, don't you know?).

The Christian concept of original sin implies that even the newborn baby is doomed to play this depressing role for his or her entire life. But don't go thinking that death will bring a release from this condemnation. Their only hope of avoiding an eternity in the fiery pit of hell is to spend this lifetime on their knees begging an angry God for forgiveness (forgiveness for things it hasn't even done). No wonder church attendances are in perpetual decline.

Let's be grown up about this; God is not the old man sitting on a cloud passing judgment on us.

God is within us, a part of our being. Essentially, we are God and God is us, and accepting this crucial principle allows divinity to flow from within us. Ironically, to even state such a thing is also considered a mortal sin in itself by traditional religions. So if you tell your priest about this book, you are 99% guaranteed to piss off the big man upstairs.

3. The illusion of labels

We tend to describe God as being a man and perhaps even picture him as having human physical form. God is not a person and has no other earthly construct. There is no height, depth, size or shape to God. God has no gender, face, hair, legs or arms. God does not reside anywhere but rather everywhere. The word God is just a label to help children apply a simple context to a principle that is confusing and beyond the comprehension of even our brightest thinkers.

The problem with labels is that they come with baggage. If I tell you to pray, you may refuse because you are not religious. However, manifesting and cosmic ordering are just other labels that mean the same thing as prayer. We tend to get wrapped up in the labels of life. If someone claims we are dishonest, we get very offended, even if it's not true.

You may think initially that positive labels are a benefit. For example it would be entirely reasonable to assume that having a reputation for being a good parent, kind nurse, dedicated son or generous friend are all positive badges for someone to wear. The label itself is not the problem but our attachment to them as some sort of false God.

Here's an extreme example for you. If I wrote a book about what a bitch Mother Teresa was, then a lot of people would get very offended and immediately jump to her defense. They would insult me and refer me to the huge amount of selfless work that she did to help others as proof that she is worthy of all the positive labels we collectively adorn her memory with. People would attack the insult because they feel attached to and secure in their beliefs about Mother Teresa.

Nobody likes to have their beliefs stolen from them, even if they are not beliefs that serve any sort of positive purpose. Millions of people around the world drink to near alcoholic levels because they believe that booze is a harmless social pleasantry. They choose to ignore the fact that alcohol is a registered poison and in the early nineties was proven beyond reasonable doubt to be a leading cause of cancer. They like their beliefs (their beliefs give them permission to drink) and they do not want to be reminded that 3.5 million people die every year as a direct result of drinking alcohol. A lot of them will get very offended if you challenge their drinking or criticize their drug (by the way, they also don't like it being called a drug).

Before we leap to the defense of Mother Teresa and her treatment at the pen of this terrible, unscrupulous author, we should ask some important questions:

- Do my insults take anything away from the amazing work she did?
- Do my claims change who she was as a person?
- Am I correct in my assertion?

If the answer to all those questions is no, then why do we waste so much energy getting angry? Shortly you will find out just how powerful that energy is, and it will confirm for you once and for all that it should never be wasted on negative pursuits such as this.

To remove the blockage caused by this third illusion, try to detach yourself from giving yourself or other people and events around you specific labels. The law of attraction works by altering your own vibrational energy to match that of the universal field of energy that flows through everything else. You can label this field God/Source/Cosmos/The Universe or Dave: it doesn't make any difference. If I call you a thief, you don't instantly become a thief as a consequence of my action, and this powerful field of energy doesn't change based on what you call it either.

4. The illusion of time

This is a tricky one to accept, but time as we generally refer to it in day-to-day life does not really exist. Time implies something linear exists in our world, a bit like watching a movie on one of those old VHS videotapes. When you insert the tape into the machine and press *play*, you watch the pre-recorded events unfold. The end of the movie already exists and if you so choose you can fast-forward the tape to a future point. Equally, if you miss a bit of the action, you can hit the rewind button and go back in 'time'. Life appears to be similar to the format of a VHS videotape because we can remember the past and we assume that there will also be a future.

However, we cannot rewind life because what happened before this precise moment does not exist anymore. We cannot fast-forward life through the bad points because the future does not exist either. If VHS movies were actually like real life, then the tape would be blank when you inserted it in the machine. The machine would create the story appearing on the screen at the moment you viewed it and then instantly erase it as soon as the image leaves the screen. At the end of the movie, the videotape would once again be completely blank.

The past and the future are virtual creations of our ego and nothing more. Everything is happening now, in this moment, and only in this moment. We have no fast-forward and no rewind buttons.

When we forget that time is just an illusion, we start trying to control aspects of reality that simply don't exist. We hope for a better future, we dream about reliving the glorious victories of our youth. These wishes will never be fulfilled because they are all located in a time period that will never be. This is not something new to people trying out the law of attraction or cosmic ordering. For thousands of years, people have been praying to God and all the time placing their requests in a time period that doesn't exist. They ask to win the lottery on Saturday, to be able to pay the bills next month or for something as general as for life to be better in the future.

When I was a child, my parents used to regularly take me and my brother to a country pub in the North East of England called the A1 (named after the famous road on which it was situated). Above the bar was a polished brass sign; it said 'All drinks free tomorrow'. Of course, the comedy being that if you come back tomorrow the sign will still say the same thing. Tomorrow and yesterday do not exist in this moment and nobody ever got a free pint of beer in that pub.

I appreciate that this illusion is the most complicated one to accept because it defies everything we have seen unfold before us. We start at birth and we struggle through life as long as we possibly can until eventually we die. It's hard to deny this is the reality because we have seen many people be born, live and then eventually pop their clogs, as the saying goes. Purely from the point of view of using the law of attraction, it is much more helpful to see this as nothing more than an illusion. The fact that you were alive yesterday and you may also be alive tomorrow has no relevance to what happens to you right here in this moment (the only moment that will ever exist). The unseen reality is that you are more like a creator choosing to manifest life second by second. Every moment that appears, you create and then destroy instantly. You do this millions of times over a lifetime.

If it makes it easier, try to view your time on earth as a period in which you experience thousands of different lives. Each day represents a new life, a new opportunity to manifest. Today cannot touch yesterday or tomorrow. It is only valid for 24 hours. Think about this: tonight you will go to sleep and while you are dreaming, your central nervous system will destroy, discard and replace millions of cells in your body. By the time you wake up tomorrow morning, a percentage of who you were today will have disappeared forever and a similar percentage of you will be taking its first ever step on planet earth in the role of you. Fast forward a few months and virtually every part of the 'you' that exists today will be gone, replaced by entirely new cells.

Let go of the past. You were not there anyway. Forget about the future. You will never get there either.

5. The illusion of scarcity

As a species we struggle with this. We even teach our children that money is hard to come by and should be saved for a rainy day. It would be better if we looked at money like water. It flows all over the planet and everywhere it goes it's useful, it makes things happen and it's passed along. We could say that water doesn't belong to any of us or that it belongs to all of us. When water is flowing and moving, it cleanses, it purifies, it makes things green, it creates growth, it nurtures. But when water starts to slow down, is held back and starts to be still, it can be toxic and stagnant to those who hold it.

Many believe that you are a better person if you are poor and that if you become rich, you also become greedy and unclean at the same time. The truth is, money doesn't really exist. Money is just traded for power and it is power that we believe corrupts, as the saying goes.

The desire for money and power comes only from fear, and fear is purely a construct of your ego. The fragment of divinity within you is not afraid of anything. Think about it, why would God be afraid of not having a car as extravagant as his neighbor's, who is also God?

Living in a scarcity mindset is a powerful block to the law of attraction and ultimately to you living a happy, peaceful and fulfilling life on earth.

6. The illusion of blame

Any excuse for your misery that points the finger of blame at someone else is a block to manifestation. Claiming you are hopeless in relationships because your parents never showed you any love as a child may or may not be true, but the act of holding onto the blame is the action that is causing you problems today.

Holding on to resentment is like holding onto a red-hot stone with the intention of throwing it at the person you blame. You are the one who gets burnt.

"You must take private responsibility. You can notice the circumstances, the seasons nor the

wind does change, only you yourself can change"
~ Jim Rohn

The most widespread misconception in contemporary times is that we firmly believe that we have a right to a fantastic, perfect life. Increasingly, we are breeding generations that are cursed with a terrible sense of entitlement. That somehow, somewhere, someone (definitely not us) enriches our lives with constant joy, interesting careers, fantastic options and a chilled family life in addition to joyous personal partnerships that only exist because we exist.

Is it not true that your parents think you are lucky because you had so much more than they did when they were growing up? If you have children, you probably now witness the same evolution of materialism unfolding again. The collective ego of the world is snowballing as our children watch the super-rich on TV every week. I am pretty sure that my daughter thinks that the Kardashians represent real life and her cruel parents are deliberately exposing her to relative poverty just to be mean.

The life you want will never be found in an external location, nor will it be delivered to you on a silver plate. The reality is that there is just one person who is accountable for the quality of your life.

That person is YOU.

If you want to succeed and accomplish your intentions, you need to take 100% responsibility for everything that happens in your life. This includes your level of efficiency, the results you generate, the quality of your relationships, your state of health and wellness and physical fitness, your salary, your debts, your emotions—everything!

The majority of us have been so conditioned, however, that we blame everybody, anything beyond our own selves for the factors in our lives that are not good. We blame our moms and dads, our educators, our boss, the Internet, our partners, the weather, politics or economics. Does pointing the finger of blame change anything in your life? Absolutely nothing. Therefore, the only thing you need to do, if you want to transform something in your life, is to take 100% responsibility for it and your feeling about it. There is no other approach.

I found the following simple formula by Jack Canfield:

E + R = O
Event + Response = Outcome

The idea is that each outcome is determined by the activity and the response. It does not matter if the outcome is success or failure, riches or scarcity, health or sickness, fun or frustration. If you believe the outcome is bad, there are only two possibilities:

A: You can choose to give the event the 'blame' for the lack of results.

Simply put, you can blame everybody: your partner, your children, the general public, your boss and the incompetence of the government or the lack of encouragement you get from your family. These factors exist, no question, but if these were the determining factors in whether you succeed or fail, then nobody would be wealthy.

Bill Gates would never have established Microsoft. Steve Jobs never would have set the megacorporation Apple rolling down the hill. Do you really think millionaires are just people who grew up with perfect parents and 100% support and encouragement? Gates and Jobs definitely have had the same conditions and became hugely successful nonetheless. You can join them, if you take responsibility.

Blaming others effectively sets yourself limitations about what you believe you can achieve. Remember, 'whether you believe you can or you believe you can't—you are right'. Apportioning blame means that you are giving up or maybe even that you are afraid of success. Lots of people leave the so-called limiting factors behind them, so it cannot be the variables that limit you. The reasons on the outside are not the ones keeping you beyond success; it is always YOU and what you believe about yourself.

We defend ourselves from responsibility even for self-destructive habits (like cigarette smoking and alcohol consumption) with inexcusable reasoning. We tell ourselves that we deserve a nice glass (or more often a bottle) of wine at the end of the day because we have worked hard. Treating ourselves to a carcinogenic glass of poison as a reward for hard work is complete insanity, but we have become so good at avoiding the truth that we can no longer see what is in front of our face.

7. The illusion of assumption

If a tree falls in a forest and there is nobody there to observe it, does it make any sound? Until very recently, my answer to this age-old question would have been *of course it does, don't be so silly*. Only recently, as I have searched for scientific evidence to back up the theories of the law of attraction, has my position changed on this. Not just changed but reversed. I am now more likely to believe that unobserved trees fall in silence. The reasons why are extremely important elements behind the theory of manifestation. I will explain in detail shortly.

Over the centuries, we have become more and more sophisticated as a species. We used to believe the earth was flat because it looked that way. We used to believe the sun revolved around the earth because from our earthly point of view, that seems to be the most logical conclusion and so we made an assumption.

Go back to Roman times or even the ancient Greeks and belief in multiple Gods was common. Today, that is roundly considered a laughably flawed theory, and the single deity has become the default position of Western religions. However, increasingly even this point of view seems too childish a concept for many to accept, and agnosticism and atheism are rapidly growing as the only logical conclusion to be drawn from the facts we are offered. Science is becoming our yardstick, faith is declining and evidence-based belief systems are becoming the mainstream. Seems sensible, right? But where this logic falls over is when we look beyond the surface and start to examine life on a particle-by-particle level.

In quantum physics, we are discovering that the elements don't obey logic and our assumptions are making an ass of you and me. Perhaps the most famous quantum research study that you will hear mentioned is what was called the 'twin slit experiment'.

To describe the twin slit experiment, consider a Ping-Pong ball firing device that shoots out Ping-

Pong balls that travel across a space and hit the wall.

Now think of the ball-firing machine being compressed down to the size of the quantum level and rather than shooting out Ping-Pong balls, it now shoots out extremely tiny particles called electrons. Those electrons pass through a vacuum and hit the wall, which marks their positions.

Now picture a small screen with a single vertical slit in the center that is positioned between the particle launcher and the wall. Many of the electrons will travel through the slit and hit the wall behind it and many will be blocked.

What we will see on the wall is a vertical column clearly showing where the electrons have hit the wall (directly behind the slit).

Next, rather than a single slit, imagine the screen contains double slits. Now the electrons can travel through either one of those slits to strike the wall behind the screen.

What we expect to see is two vertical columns marking the region where the electrons pass through on slit or the other and make impact with the wall. But the peculiar and amazing thing is that we do not witness what we assumed would happen. Instead what we see are several vertical columns a small distance apart from one another appearing on the wall.

Imagine a swimming pool partitioned by a screen. This screen has two slits in the center exactly the same as I just described for our lab-based experiment. When an object is dropped into the pool in front of the twin slit partition, it causes a circular wave to ripple outward in every direction. The surge travels through the twin slits and divides into two smaller waves. As the two ripples continue to travel, they simultaneously reinforce and counteract each other at certain angles.

What you observe on the wall at the end are numerous vertical columns, each spread a minimal amount apart from the next. The columns show where the waves bolster one another, while the spaces demonstrate where the waves cancel each other out.

monochromatic planar wave (e.g. a laser)

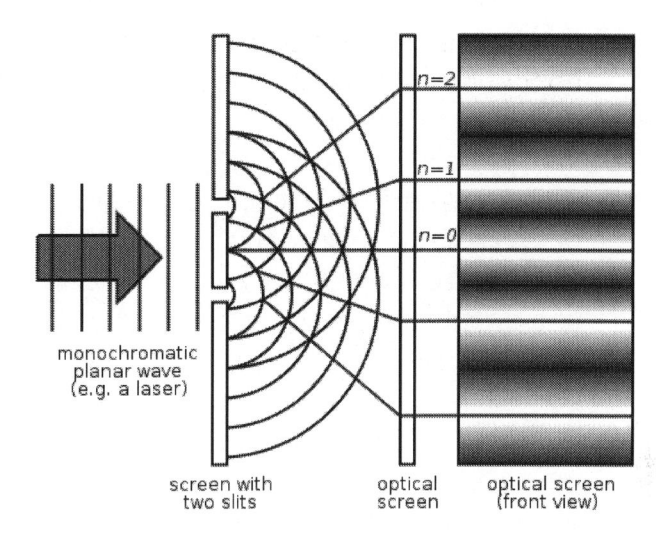

screen with two slits

optical screen

optical screen (front view)

So the question is why does the electron act like a wave when it passes through the double apertures?

The theory is that the electron splits into two when it reaches the screen and travels through both holes at the same time. It then disrupts itself, consequently causing a wave effect that creates the multiple lines on the rear wall. In quantum physics, this is called the theory of non-locality, which is the theory that an element exists in two locations at one time. It is not limited to one place in time and space but it becomes universal.

The scientists were fairly certain in their assumption that the multiple lines were being created by the particles creating a wave. So to confirm their hypothesis a tiny device was positioned in front of the double slits in the screen so that they could observe what occurs when the electron penetrates it.

The outcome they got was unusual beyond ordinary explanation. This time, what they saw on the rear wall was just two vertical columns instead of the multiple ones that they had witnessed initially.

This was a complete head-scratcher for the logically minded scientists because what it showed was that when they were watching, a particle acted like a particle. However, when they were not looking, the particles acted like a wave. The scientists struggled to accept this, because it appeared that 2+2=9.

This is very confusing for scientists but it is a beautiful thing for authors like me. I have witnessed my life being completely turned around by something I know to be real. It is my unwavering belief in the law of attraction that makes it work so well for me. Bully for me, but if I want to use this knowledge to help other people, then it is unrealistic to simply demand that they believe 100% in what I am saying. I appreciate that no matter how much you may want to believe me, there is always going to be an eyebrow raised here or there to certain parts of this phenomenon. At times you are going to think 'this is too good to be true'.

I am excited because the double slit experiment allows me to apply logic to something entirely illogical.

Quantum physicists talk about electrons or events being potential rather than being real physical entities. Nothing is solid but rather a liquid of various potentialities, essentially until somebody looks, and then the looking sort of forces the universe to make a determination about which possibility is going to be realized. All of reality is effectively a limitless quantum field of energy, an ocean of boundless opportunities waiting to transpire.

It sounds impossible, but what I am saying to you really is that I believe the tree makes no sound when it falls unless you are there to make the measurement. Your thoughts are the energy that makes the sound; if you are not present, there is no energy and ergo no sound. When you observe life, you automatically generate thoughts and your thoughts create waves of energy that alter reality. Right at the start of this book I told you that you have the power to manifest the life of your dreams and I hope by now you are starting to get excited that this might actually be a very real and tangible reality.

Consciousness is the fuel that alters energy. All energy is actually consciousness; therefore, it is consciousness guiding itself. The observer is not apart from the observation. The experimenter is not apart from the experiment.

Everything is energy and energy is everything. What this experiment proves is that you are the universe and the universe is you. Without your thoughts and interaction, the universe does not exist. Essentially you have a limited but beautiful choice to make. You can sit back and observe life and thereby send out your submissive observational energy waves and accept what comes back (living a reactionary life—like the vast majority of human beings), or you can decide now to take control of the energy that you are emitting into the universe and start designing the outcome you receive back. The only choice you can't make is to opt out of this process. Whatever thoughts you create are going to have an impact on your life and on the universe as a whole, so why not be in the driver's seat rather than live like most people do, as a mere blindfolded passenger.

It's too good to be true

It was always my intention that *Millionaire Mindset* would be a practical book that could be quickly understood and applied to your life. I have tried my best to avoid the author's license to flannel and padding. Whether I have succeeded or not will be entirely subjective, I have no doubt. Shortly, I will give you very clear instructions about how you can start manifesting the life of your dreams. If you are 100% certain that what I have told you so far is true, then feel free to skip ahead to the section entitled 'The 421 Journal'. However, if there are thoughts of 'this all sounds too good to be true' buzzing around your conscious mind, I want to take a moment to address those thoughts now.

I consider myself a relatively intelligent guy with enough street smarts to successfully dodge all scams and scammers that have so far taken me on as a potential mug. I do not believe in fairies, leprechauns, the tooth fairy or Father Christmas. I find most conspiracy theories rather tedious and as such I do not believe 9/11 was anything but a terrorist attack and that the white lines you see in the skies (dubbed chem trails) are the government attempting surreptitiously to poison the common people but rather that they are the simple result of high-temperature exhaust fumes hitting super cold air. My father was a butcher from the North East of England and I consider my heritage to be from a no-nonsense working-class family background. I do not write this sort of material lightly or without pure and total conviction that what I am telling you is true. If my parents were old hippies called Tarquin and Jeminah and we loved nothing more than to spend our summers in the woods dancing around a campfire naked, then I would advise you to take my words with extreme caution.

I do not believe in blind faith. If I am told something, I expect to be able to replicate the results I have been informed about or I will discard the notion. The law of attraction has changed my life beyond all recognition, and I want you to experience the state of bliss that I feel right now. This section of the book is designed to answer the (quite logical) questions of naturally skeptical people everywhere. Sensible, grounded people who really want to believe, but for whom there is just a smattering of 'too good to be true' still lingering. I have tried to answer the most frequent questions I am asked on this subject, but if I miss the element that is most causing you puzzlement, please do email me from the website and I will do my very best to give you a comprehensive answer.

Q1. If the law of attraction is real, why don't I see it happening around me all the time?

You do, but you probably don't currently identify it as the law of attraction at work. There is a perfect example of the universe delivering dreams happening here in England at this very moment. I am writing this section of the book in the business lounge of Manchester Airport on Sunday 1st of May 2016. The city of Manchester is preparing for big crowds to descend on it later this afternoon when the players and fans of Leicester City football club arrive to play a crucial soccer match against the world-famous Manchester United. If you are not a follower of British soccer, let me explain that the Leicester City squad of players have an estimated value of around £31,000,000, a lot of money but peanuts by the standards of some clubs. They will be playing the Manchester United team, whose value is thought to be over £340,000,000. If this were Formula One, it would be like racing Michael Schumacher's Ferrari F2004 against a Ford Fiesta. If Leicester beat Man United today (and I believe they will), they will win the league, if they lose they will still win the league but it will take another week. Regardless of what happens today, Leicester City will end the season significantly higher up the table than the likes of Manchester United, a team worth over ten times more than them.

If you had placed a bet at the start of the soccer season on this outcome, the bookmakers would have laughed you out of the shop. Odds available for this bet were 5000/1. If you are not familiar with sports gambling, allow me to explain. When odds get over 1000/1, it is the bookmaker quite clearly saying this is not going to happen. For instance, you can probably get odds of 10000/1 that Elvis will be found alive and well and running a fish and chip shop in London. Leicester don't have the best players, they don't have the best coaching staff, they don't have the best training facilities and they don't have anywhere near the financial resources of the other clubs, and yet they will beat every other team in the league this year. I suppose you could claim that Leicester City got lucky and perhaps you could point to two or three games and label it good fortune, but the Premiership season is long and hard. You would have to be pretty convinced of the power of luck to claim that this team were just lucky in all 38 games that they played to reach this point.

Our thoughts have energy and when we deeply believe and focus on our desires, we send out immense and powerful waves of this energy. What do you think happens when 100,000 fans all believe the same thing? This is what we call the collective will and it can move mountains. David killed Goliath because he believed, he saw the victory before it happened and sent the corresponding wave of energy into the ether (or if you want the dumbed down explanation, a miracle happened —thank the Lord).

It is worth being aware that the collective will of society can also create devastatingly bad outcomes. Consider World War II for instance; it is a little too easy to point the entire finger of blame at Adolf Hitler. Realistically, one man could not do that much damage on his own. Most of the German people were largely unaware of the true horrific extent of the atrocities being committed in their names, but there were still enough people willing to build, run or just plain ignore the concentration camps on their doorsteps. Camps similar to Auschwitz, where millions of men, women and children were systematically starved, tortured and murdered.

Adolf Hitler wasn't initially a dictator imposing his will on a helpless nation; the people of the time voted him into power. His hard line resonated with the feelings of the downtrodden majority in the country. Germany had been completely humiliated in the First World War and the punishment handed down by the allied nations brought the Germans to their knees. The country was rendered bankrupt and all hope of recovery was pointless due to heavy fines and debts imposed on the country by the rest of Europe. If the situation hadn't changed dramatically,

Germany would have been still paying their debts to the allies well into 1987. The country was in a bitter depression with no jobs and no opportunities, and hyperinflation had made the currency next to worthless. In 1922, a loaf of bread in Germany would have cost you 160 marks. One year later, the same loaf of bread cost 200,000,000,000 marks. You literally couldn't carry all the money to the baker that you would need to buy the bread.

The collective mind-set of the people was that of a deep inner resentment that they were being bullied and harshly treated and it was time to stand up and fight back against the bullies. The result of this miserable national state of mind is written in blood in our history books.

Q2. Why can't I do something simple to prove it works, like placing a winning bet on a sports event?

The problem with this concept as a test is that there are too many unknown variables. Let's take a horse race as an example. Imagine there are six runners and you have put a small bet on horse number five, just to test this law of attraction business. What you don't know is how many other people are betting on the other horses and how many of them are also firing their own rockets of intention into the universe. There might be a guy across town wagering his last penny on horse number 2. He is on his knees begging for a result because anything less than a win is going to mean he can't pay his rent and will lose his home. In this situation, your win would cause him significant harm (and you would never know anything about it). You can't ask the universe to manifest harm to other people because divinity is love and love has nothing to do with the array of negative emotions we experience as a part of the human condition.

The second thing I have noticed is that the universe ignores your insistence on when something arrives. Time as we know it is an irrelevant concept to the cosmos. I have found the universe is very similar to Cypriots; it is not in a rush to do anything—tomorrow is just fine thank you very much. Most of the time when you ask for something, you are completely unaware of all the elements that have to come together to make it happen. I could state my intention that I want to see the earth from space just once in my lifetime. I am sure you can see how this could be possible if the right events happen in the correct order. If I demand that I become an astronaut by this afternoon, I am backing the universe into a corner—it doesn't have the material to work with in order to give me what I want. Remember, your intentions need to be for amazing things that are beneficial (or at the very least, that do no harm) to everyone involved.

Finally, I believe you are communicating via a divine fragment of your eternal being. This part of you knows why you are here and what you really should be doing with your life. If you won one horse race, the chances are good you would place another larger bet, and before long this trivial activity would become your obsession. I am reasonably certain that your purpose in life is not just to teach the bookmaker a lesson or two. Giving you what you want in this case could cause a domino effect that destroys your life. The universe will ignore you if you try to cause harm, even if the harm is only to yourself. Remember, the illusion of separation means that it is not possible to contain the harm only to yourself. The damage you inflict on yourself will create a ripple of negative energy that impact others far and wide.

Q3. If we are as powerful and divine as you say, then why do so many bad things happen and why can't we stop them?

The hitch with this question is that it comes from within the illusion of God. It assumes we are silly children and we need to be supervised for our own good. The problem is that there is no greater power that can be asked to keep an eye on us, we are God—you can't go any higher. How would you feel if I said to you that you can't be trusted to drive a car safely and I am going to have someone else supervise all your future driving. Most people would be highly insulted and offended at the very suggestion. But only because mostly we all think we are very good drivers—it's the guy in the car in front of us who is a bloody idiot.

When you become experienced at tapping into the power of the universe and you reach the point where I am, when you believe with 100% conviction that the rockets you launch into the universe will hit their target, and while you may not know exactly how the intention will be delivered, but you do know with certainty that something beautiful is on the way, *then* you will feel the confidence and self-belief in your own freewill that you already feel about your ability to drive a car.

Q4. I asked the universe to let me find my soulmate but I keep ending up in bad relationships with the wrong people—what gives?

Here we have another question phrased from within the illusion of time. So you want to meet your soulmate? But, presumably you don't want to meet them and then completely mess it up and scare them away?

Of course not, so maybe you need to learn a few lessons first? Do not place timescales on your intentions; trust the universe to deliver your dreams when it is perfect for you and your soul mate and not a moment too early or too late. Maybe you are ready but your partner needs a few more lessons, or vice versa. If I had met Daniela five years ago, I would have still fallen instantly head over heels in love with her, but I know for a fact that I was not the man she needed me to be at that point. Our relationship would have been short, dramatic and very painful.

Just like your future relationship with your soul mate, your relationship with the universe should be built on a rock-solid foundation of trust and love.

Q5. If I worry about negative things, will I manifest them into my life?

You don't need to worry; your fleeting predictions of doom and gloom won't be manifested unless you go to great effort to apply your focus on them in a dedicated manner. If you spend four hours a day visualizing a terrible car crash then you are likely to be operating at a very low vibrational state and pulling negativity towards you, but it doesn't necessarily mean you will crash your car that week. If we only had to think of something and it would magically appear, we would have aircraft crashing all over the place, lions escaping from zoos every day and bosses dropping down dead every time they chastised an employee who was late for work.

Trust me on this, if you follow the guide I am about to explain to you, nothing but amazing events and people will be turning up in your life very soon.

The 421 Journal

Most people meander through life without bothering to write down their goals. Very few people have specific and measurable goals, and even fewer have written these goals down. An even smaller number have also thought of a specific plan to make these goals a reality.

But does writing down your goals really help, or is it just a myth? If it really helps, what's the best goal-setting strategy?

Forbes reports a remarkable study about goal-setting carried out in the Harvard MBA program. Harvard's graduate students were asked whether they had set clear, written goals for their futures, as well as whether they had made specific plans to transform their fantasies into realities.

The result of the study was that only 3% of the students had written goals and plans to accomplish them, 13% had goals in their minds but hadn't written them anywhere, and 84% had no goals at all.

After 10 years, the same group of students were interviewed again and the conclusion of the study was totally astonishing.

- The 13% of the class who had goals, but did not write them down, earned twice the amount of the 84% who had no goals.

- The 3% who had written goals were earning, on average, ten times as much as the other 97% of the class combined.

- People who don't write down their goals tend to fail more easily than people who have plans.

There is power in the pen, but it is not so much the fact that you have your wishes and desires written down but rather that you paused your busy life for a moment to focus 100% on thinking about what you want. Sure, you can daydream about what you want to manifest while you are making a cup of coffee, but how much of your focus is on the desire and how much is on not scalding yourself with the boiling water? When you sit down with a journal and a pen and think carefully about what you want in your life, it requires your sole concentration, or perhaps I should say your soul concentration.

You may have read other law of attraction books that water down the principle of this universal law into 'you get what you think about'. A lot of people try this and quickly become despondent when their dreams don't start showing up. Others manage some initial success but then lose momentum; the magic appears to wear off. This is all because the law of attraction is not so simple that you just have to think about what you want and it miraculously appears, and thank God it isn't. You would be having lions and tigers and bears turning up in your living room all the time if this were true, oh my!

The easiest way I can explain this to you is by asking you to imagine that we are all vessels or containers, similar to a water jug. If you start pouring water into the jug, there will quickly come a point at which the jug is full and no more water can be added. At this point you are left with two choices: you can leave the jug as it is, but in doing so allow the water to go stagnant, or you can pour some of the water out to make room for more to be added. It is the same with us, but instead of water, imagine the substance we contain is the power of the universe. If you constantly keep asking for more and more stuff to appear in your life, you will get to a point where your connection to source becomes stagnant. You will stop manifesting the life you desire because there simply isn't any more room in your vessel.

To live this beautiful life I am teaching about, you must be like a river and not like a dam. Love, money, success and happiness must be constantly flowing through your life. You can't expect to manifest your soulmate and then treat him or her badly. For you to find your perfect partner, the love you receive must be equal to the love you give. Otherwise the relationship will stagnate for one or both of you. This principle applies to everything you manifest using the law of attraction. If you hoard the extra money you create using the secrets of this book, eventually the universe will stop responding to your requests for more wealth. You will have become a blockage in the flow of money; source becomes aware that once money gets to you, it goes no further.

To ensure you get the balance right, I have spent a lot of time working on a way that you can always ensure you give back to source in sufficient quantity so that there is always water flowing into your vessel. Every morning I sit down with a cup of coffee and I open a very beautiful leather-bound notepad. Clipped to the side of this pad is a wonderfully elegant silver fountain pen. This daily diary is called my 421 Journal. If you are really serious about changing your life, I am suggest you do the same thing every day. Today go and buy a notepad and pen. I find it adds to the routine if you put a little care and attention into the writing materials you are going to be using. Buy a beautiful notebook and a pen that you like to write with. This routine is going to be an important and magical part of your day, so make sure it feels significant.

The number 421 refers to the balance of giving, sending and receiving you are going to be offering to the universe every day. It is important that you find a moment of peace and tranquility every day where you can do this. Your focus needs to be completely on the page. If the children are running around the kitchen while you are trying to write or your secretary keeps calling you at your desk, then your attention is broken. For example, this morning I got up at 5:30 am, long before my kids get up for school. I fed the dogs and cats and made myself a cup of coffee. Then I sat in silence and opened my journal. I already knew what I was going to write because I had awoken a few times during the night with thoughts that I instantly decided needed to be in my diary for today.

At the top of a new page I wrote today's date, 29th April 2016. Next I started to write out four statements of things in my life that I am profoundly grateful for. I am away from my home in Cyprus at the moment, and I woke up to an SMS message from my partner Daniela that simply said "Good morning, I love you'. So the first line of my journal today states 'Thank you for the amazing loving relationship that Daniela and I enjoy so much'.

Next I write down two things in my awareness that need more love. I sent my love to my daughter, who is having a tough time at school at the moment, and also to a friend who today will have a biopsy on his lung to check for cancer.

Finally, I wrote down my intention for today, or if you prefer, my instruction to the universe of what I want delivered. This doesn't have to be an earth-shatteringly large request; it can be big or small. A steady stream of small manifestations is much more rewarding than taking risks with gigantic requests to win the lottery, etc. I have some good news and some bad news for you about this whole law of attraction thing. The bad news is that this is not Aladdin's lamp. You can't wish for anything and WHOOSH it magically appears. Imagine if ten thousand people bought this book and all on the same day they wrote 'I want to win the lottery today'. How can the universe generate that many winning tickets? And even if it did, the prize pool would be divided so many times that every single person would be left disappointed. You are asking the universe to push you in a direction rather than just hand stuff to you on a silver plate. If you ask to meet your soul mate, the universe will not create a new person from scratch (like in that *Weird Science movie*), but rather it will start moving two compatible people closer together, motivating you both to be at the same place at the same time and so on.

So you have had the bad news; now for the good. Unlike Aladdin's lamp you don't get just three wishes—you get 365 wishes. One a day for every day of the year. Before you ask... yes, you can ask for more than that, but I have found it is better to focus your intention on one a day. Otherwise you get lost in perpetually 'wanting'. When this happens, blockages start appearing. The 421 Journal is designed to put your primary focus on giving rather than on receiving. Each day's entry starts with four expressions of gratitude for what you already have in your life, two gifts of love for someone else and one cosmic order to the universe.

You will come to see this journal as something quite magical in your life, a sacred document. When I sit down to write in my own 421 Journal, I take the process very seriously. I make sure I am in a quiet place on my own, and before I put pen to paper I sit in silent contemplation for a few moments. I know that what I write in that book will become reality, so it is worth pausing just for a moment and focusing on what would serve me best. There is no doubt in my mind that what I have asked for will be delivered, I know that the moment the intention is set, the outcome has already happened—even before the ink dries. All I have to do next is wait patiently for time to catch up. It's a bit like sending an ethereal email—once you click send you can't see where the message is on its journey, and you don't worry about which part of the Internet is currently hosting your communication. As soon as you click send an unbreakable chain of events begins. If you have ever sent an email to entirely the wrong (and most inappropriate) person, then you will know firsthand that it doesn't matter how many times you click cancel. That disastrous message has already delivered its payload.

Joining The 20%

"Do the difficult things while they are easy and do the great things while they are small. A journey of a thousand miles must begin with a single step", Lao Tzu

Millionaires are proactive by nature and this is perhaps one of the most striking differences you can notice between the 20% and the 80%. Most people are simply reacting to the hand that they are dealt, mainly because they believe this is the only option available. Living a reactionary life like this means a person is essentially a boat in the ocean without a rudder or any means of population. Even if they spot dangerous rocks on the horizon they feel powerless to do anything but sit and hope they get lucky. However, for the most part they are completely unaware of the rocks until they hit them and then they feel hard done to and wonder why they are being punished by life.

Most people are sheep not wolves and they default to the comfort zone setting of living a reactive life. This is understandably because our brains are hardwired to protect us from dangerous situations. This is a throw back to our hunter-gatherer days when danger and life threatening events were around each and every corner. Civilization has progressed in the western world but evolution has not kept up pace. The risk assessment areas of our brain are a little over zealous for the new environment in which we live. Being afraid to approach a sleeping lion is a perfect example of where fear is being generated to serve a valuable purpose. However, feeling that exact same sense of dread about following your dreams is an inappropriate sensation and does not serve us in any positive way. Actually, many people would rather approach a snoozing lion and flick it hard on the nose than step out of the comfort of their daily routine.

The part of our brain that generates this powerful motivating force would rather we always default to our comfort zone. The comfort zone is safe and requires less work to remain in it. For example would you feel more relaxed walking around your own home in a power blackout or in a huge ancient castle in the middle of nowhere? Of course home is the obvious choice because you find comfort in the familiar surroundings, you know where everything you need is and you also know how to get out of there if you had to. Simply put your brain is pushing you to stay safely at home to avoid the risks of the unknown… always!

While the fear of truly committing to your goals feels very real, you need to be aware that it is a subjective illusion, by that I mean the same situation can appear different if viewed from another angle. Our beliefs are much more powerful than we give them credit for. We can literally manifest reality from our beliefs. I loved the story Zig Ziglar used to tell to demonstrate this point:

At the airport, a woman with plenty of hours to spare before her flight went to buy a book and a bag of cookies in the shops inside the airport. She then found a place to sit and started reading. She was so absorbed in reading her book and yet, she still noticed a man take a cookie from the bag between them.

She continued with the cookies and ignored the man to avoid any scene. Soon, the cookie thief diminished her stock until only one was left. The man laughed nervously, took the last cookie and broke it in two pieces. Then he offered the half to her and ate the other half.
The woman snatched the other half of the cookie. She thought how rude that man was. He never even thanked her! And she could not remember a time when she had been so agitated.

And so she was relieved when her flight was called, she took all her belongings and went to the gate. On her way out, she did not bother to look at the cookie thief.
When she was comfortably seated, she took out her book to read again and to her surprise, found her cookies inside her bag. Then the realization hit her, he shared his cookies with her and she was the cookie thief all along!

Sometime we become so convinced that what we think we see and feel is real that we become paralyzed by it. When I first moved to the island of Cyprus I couldn't believe how rude and impolite the Greek Cypriots were. I couldn't even drive to the supermarket without getting cut up on the highway or being aggressively tailgated all the way to the store. People were constantly cutting in line and the people serving me in stores would never smile or offer any politeness. For quite a while I firmly held the belief that the Cypriots were a very rude bunch of people indeed. Then I made a couple of friends who were born and bred in Cyprus. I became good friends with the owner of the local pharmacy, a very wise and friendly guy called Savvas. Shortly after meeting him he took me out to lunch and for three hours we shared good food and conversation. For most of the time he sang the praises of Cyprus and it's people. He told me that I was a very lucky guy because I had the good fortune to live in Cyprus, home to very loving and compassionate people. Savvas insisted that I could spend the rest of my days travelling the world and I would never find more caring people than the Cypriots. Of course I didn't challenge his beliefs, but let's just say I wasn't entirely on board with what he was saying.

But then something strange happened. Over the next few weeks I noticed a dramatic change in the Cypriots. They became better drivers, shop assistants started smiling, strangers in the street started to wish me a good morning as I walked passed them. There are only two explanations for this paradigm shift, either the whole country of Cyprus had a secret meeting and agreed to be a bit more hospitable or more likely the change I was witnessing wasn't out there but rather it was inside me.

Life is a big boomerang, be careful what you throw out there because it's all coming back to you and at speed. This principle is so important that I refer to it as a law. What I mean by this is, it doesn't matter whether you agree with it or not – it's going to happen regardless of your views. In the same way that the law of gravity doesn't care whether you believe in it or not.

I have a friend on Facebook who if I cut and paste all her status updates here for you to read you would think 'the poor girl, what a terrible life she has'. At first glance I would admit she does appear to have extraordinary bad luck but when you take into consideration the boomerang law it all becomes entirely understandable and entirely predictable. If she has to visit the doctor her status will be along the lines of "Wish me luck I am going back to the doctor this afternoon. It will be just my luck that the test results are not even ready yet LOL". Can you guess what her next status update says? I will give you a clue, delete the LOL and replace it with FFS and you will be getting close to the theme of the status.

If you expect the doctor to mess up your consultation you send a manifestation rocket into the universe that this is what you want. If you concentrate on how crappy your marriage is and what a terrible wife or husband you have, can you see how that becomes more and more the reality. Rarely do you wake up and suddenly your marriage is fine again. We have a machine in our head with the power of creation, it's like a manifestation ray gun and whatever you point it at comes into your life. Point it at misery and it traps a load of miserable events in its tractor beam and drags them all closer to you. Point the gun at success or happiness and your life changes in the very best way.

I have read hundreds of personal development books where I get to the end and think 'yes very good, but now what'? I want this book to be a practical step-by-step manual that has a dramatic and noticeable affect on your life. In order for you to make progress you need to take action. Sticking firmly to the beautiful rules of seven I have made this super simple for you. What follows are the seven essential steps you need to take in order to leave the 80% behind and join the financial elite.

Step One: Take responsibility

You create everything you become aware of and only you can either give gratitude for that thing or clean it, if it is causing pain (for you or another). Everything you label good and bad about your life has been created by the divine power of your subconscious and soul. Essentially because you are a fragment of God you have the power of God, but unfortunately your ego interferes and causes big problems. It is a bit like giving a twelve year old the keys to a two hundred mile an hour Lamborghini and asking him not to crash it.

As the ego continually struggles to avoid fear and gain pleasure it inadvertently passes erroneous programs to the subconscious. As this part of you doesn't judge or question, it simply runs the program and before you know what is happening a whole heap of misery is being delivered into your life. It seems entirely illogical that you would create such pain for yourself and so you start looking for someone else to blame. This principle applies to everything in your life and the life of those around you.

- *If you are overweight and unhappy about the size and shape of your body then you must accept that you are responsible for creating this situation. You can no longer blame your genes, big bones, the proximity of the donut shop to your place of work or your parents.*

- *If your friend is having money trouble – this is your responsibility. I do not mean you have to bail her out or beat yourself up and feel equally as miserable as they do but you must accept that your awareness of it means it exists within you.*

- *Your boss is being a jerk and making your life miserable at work. His behaviour is your responsibility.*

I will say again… accepting 100% responsibility does not mean all these things are your fault. The concept of fault becomes irrelevant at the point we give up on the blame game. It might sound crazy, or just plain metaphorical, that the world is your creation. But if you look carefully, you will realize that whatever you call the world and perceive as the world is your world, it is the projection of your own mind.

If you go to a party you can see how in the same place, with the same light, the same people, the same food, drink, music and atmosphere, some will enjoy themselves while others will be bored, some will be overenthusiastic and some depressed, some will be talkative and others will be silent.

The "out there" for every one of them seems the same, but if one were to connect their brains to machines, immediately it would show how different areas of the brain would come alive, how different perceptions there are from one person to the next. So even if they apparently share it, the "out there" is not the same for them, let alone their inner world, their emotions.

Step Two: Dream Big & Fail Big

Dare to dream the big dream and never be tempted to dilute your goals. Back when I ran radio stations for a living I was always involved in the creative side of the business, the stuff that came out of the speakers essentially. However, because I was in a management position I would attend the weekly sales meeting. I noticed a recurring theme. The month would always start with an impressive sales target and all the execs would optimistically report that they were expecting to have a 'good month'. Around two weeks into the month, the sales executives would start to tell stories of deals slipping out of their reach, people with the authority to sign orders being on vacation and other excuses as to why they were not quite 'where they need to be'. By the third week in the month it would start to become clear that the radio station was going to miss it's sales target. So what would the manager do? They would take the path of least resistance of course and reduce the sale target. They would do this to prevent the team becoming depressed and losing passion because they failed to hit target.

This happened at least nine or ten months out of the year. In my opinion, constantly moving the goal posts closer can only work if your sales team is brainless. That sort of stuff doesn't even work on children once get passed say five or six years of age. I remember playing football with my son when he was little, of course I would always let him score a goal every now and again just to keep his enthusiasm up. I remember one time we walking home from the park and he looked miserable. "Hey, what's with the grumpy face?", I asked, "You beat your dad, you should be pretty happy with that".

"It doesn't count, you let me win", he said.

Moving the goals posts closer doesn't work because it sends out the message that the first goal was unimportant to begin with. We shouldn't be afraid to fail because if we remove the possibility of failing we rob a person of his or her opportunity to learn. Have big dreams and accept the two outcomes that will ultimately come from them, you will either have amazing and beautiful successes or painful learning experiences. We don't want anything in the middle, and I will tell you why this applies to every part of your life:

The middle (or the average) is where the 80% live or dream of living. Ask someone who is on $30,000 a year how much of a pay rise they would need to be really happy, really comfortable and they will probably state an increase between fifty and eighty percent. But this is not a big dream and will only keep you anchored in the demographic they say they want to leave. Try living in a major city like New York or London on $60,000 a year and you will find out how it feels to be middle class and poor at the same time. Very few people on $30,000 a year would set a goal of $300,000 and yet they will answer in the positive if asked if they would like to be rich. Hopefully you can see they have a counterbalancing outlook of life that is unlikely to work out in the long run.

I want you to have the sort of goals that other people tell you are ridiculous or outrageous. This should be your benchmark as to whether they are big enough. Your goals should be so grand that they almost offend people. So as a little exercise, think of the person in your life who has the most pessimistic outlook. Imagine telling them that your goal is to own three thousand apartments. See the outrage on their face and then smiled to yourself because this means you are on the right track.

Step Three: Stop taking advice off the 80%

When I was a teenager I told my father that I wanted to be a broadcaster. He told me that was a ridiculous idea and I should grow up and get a proper career with prospects. I ignored him and did what I knew I was being called to do. I ended up spending a decade as a major market broadcaster and then another decade running radio stations. At this point I told my father that I was going to quit my job and become a full time author. Again he told me I was being stupid. He advised me that it would be pure insanity to give up a good job to do something that I have no experience of doing. He chastised me for not being a happy with what I had. He told me that most people would do anything for the career and lifestyle I had. I was to stop being so selfish and ungrateful and get on with my job, before my company got wind of my ideas.

I probably don't need to tell you what happened next because if things hadn't worked out I would not be writing this book. I am not saying ignore all advice, because sometimes you need a third party opinion to clear the fog. But you must be aware that the default position of the people who love and care for you is one of 'be careful'. Parents hope their children will work hard and get a nice, safe and secure career because they don't want them to suffer hardship. Rarely do parents encourage their children to throw caution to the wind and follow their dream. When I told my father that I was going to quit my well-paid job to do what my heart was telling me to do, he responded to protect me, not to hold me back. But regardless of his motives if I had ignored my gut and taken his advice I would be miserable now. Securely employed with a regular income, sure, but miserable all the same.

You wouldn't accept investment advice from a penniless financial advisor, or weight loss advice from an obese doctor. If your goal is to get into the 20% elite then don't look to people in the 80% for wisdom, they don't have any.

Step Four: Become Obsessed

Obsession may sound like a negative trait but it's really not. Sensible, middle of the road goals deliver sensible, middle of the road outcomes. People have a predisposition to focus on what they need more than what they want. If you are $100 short of money just before payday then you may have a tendency to say 'I need $100' but this is not true. If I gave you the $100 you would probably still end the month broke. What you really need is $1000 or $10000 but sadly we are unlikely to think like this as a default response to what life throws at us.

The whole point of this book is to change your mindset. To force a paradigm shift that breaks your normal routine. Especially the commonplace routine, that money is something that is earned Monday to Friday, selling your time for cash. If you are not doing what you are here to do then I am almost certain your soul will be already trying to tell you. If you have a deep and constant sensation that something is missing in your life, if you feel like there is a vacuum inside you and nothing you do makes it go away then this is the voice of your soul, trying to push you in a different direction.

Find your passion and then become obsessed about it. Seriously if you are sitting in front of the television complaining to your husband or wife about not having enough money then you don't deserve a single dollar more than you already have. Your passion doesn't fit inside a box you label as 'work'; it is an all-consuming part of your existence. It is why you get up in the morning; it is why you breathe in and out. Unless you feel like that about what you are currently doing to earn money then you will never escape the 80%. I didn't take my friend up on his sock empire because I knew in my heart I would not be jumping out of bed in the morning to go sell more socks. You may think that is a silly example and socks are not a very sexy business for anyone to get into but trust me there are plenty of millionaires out there who made their money in much less exotic businesses than socks. It doesn't matter what anyone else thinks about your product or idea, just so long as you consider it to be your baby and give it all the love and passion you have inside yourself.

Step Five: Pay Yourself First

Before you even see you salary between 15% and 30% should be automatically removed and invested. Even if you are not in the position to save that much at the moment at least get started and begin the habit of a lifetime. As soon as you can get started, give away 5% to 10% of you money to worthy cause to embed the fluid mindset you need to have about wealth and abundance.

Step Six: Make Friends With Fear

What I have discovered in life is that pretty much anything worth having is slightly just outside your comfort zone. Whether it's launching your own business, winning the league in your chosen sport, getting the career you have dreamed of all your life or ending up with the man or woman who makes you think you just won the lottery every moment you are with them. None of these things are inside your comfort zone, they all require you to stretch and grow before you can reach them. As most people know the walls of your comfort zone are made of a very strong material called fear. In order to smash through these barriers you have to stare fear straight in the eyes and charge ahead regardless.

Fear (false evidence appearing real) is just an illusion, and I don't just mean certain types of fear. You might quite reasonably argue that the anxiousness you feel when you stand on the top of a tall building is a very valuable sensation to experience in that moment. Of course, sometimes fear serves you in the short term but the biggest problem we have, as an intelligent species is we believe that we have something to lose. Nothing helps me make this point better than my all time favorite quote by the late, great Steve Jobs:

"Remembering that I'll be dead soon is the most important tool I've ever encountered to help me make the big choices in life.

Almost everything--all external expectations, all pride, all fear of embarrassment or failure - these things just fall away in the face of death, leaving only what is truly important.

Remembering that you are going to die is the best way I know to avoid the trap of thinking you have something to lose. You are already naked. There is no reason not to follow your heart.

No one wants to die. Even people who want to go to heaven don't want to die to get there. And yet, death is the destination we all share. No one has ever escaped it, and that is how it should be, because death is very likely the single best invention of life. It's life's change agent. It clears out the old to make way for the new", Steve Jobs

Yes, it's true! You are going to die, not one of us is getting out of this alive. One day everything you ever worried about will become irrelevant dust. You are already naked, you always have been and there is not a single reason why you should not be following your dreams and living a life full of happiness, peace and purpose!

When this ride is over nobody is going to mention the day you risked it all and unsuccessfully went after that big promotion at work, nobody will recall the day you threw caution to the wind and gambled with rejection by approaching that beautiful girl you saw in the street. All this stuff is only significant to your own ego. Remember this, the 80% listen to their ego; the 20% listen to their soul. So start to see fear not as a reason to back down but as an indicator that an opportunity to grow has presented itself.

Step Seven: Invest in Yourself

You bought this book; this automatically puts you in a very select bunch of people. Virtually everyone you know wants to become rich and virtually everyone you know won't do a single thing about it. One of the most powerful things you can give yourself is to subscribe to a theory called Automobile University. If you are not earning you should at least be learning. We have so many opportunities to gain knowledge and we squander the vast majority of them. Millionaires and the 20% don't watch much TV, a significant proportion of them won't watch any at all. If you are serious about stepping up in this life then there is never again going to be time in your life for pointless reality TV shows and soap operas. Now it's important to remember that Information isn't power, it's potential power. If you don't do anything with it, then it is useless... but you do need it there in the first place.

There was some research done that shows that if you listen to an educational, motivational or success tape on the way into work in the car every day and then you listen to another tape on the way home from work, every day. Within three years you will have learnt as much as a two-year university course.

Put the good stuff in your head. Listen to these tapes and learn. Get the advantage over other people. Learn about psychology, wealth, success, happiness and good health. Buy the audiobooks, invest in them and listen to them over and over in your car. You will learn a massive amount, much more than you are consciously aware of. If you can commit to making this learning by osmosis a habit, powerful and dramatic things will start happening to you.

If you are interested in taking what you have learned in this book to the next level then make sure you checkout my Millionaire Coaching Program at www.PowerfullyWealthy.com

Thank you for reading Millionaire Mindset. I am extremely grateful that you give me a platform to share my views like this and if you wouldn't mind going back to the online store where you bought it from and giving me a rating and review I would be eternally appreciative for your help in spreading this work as far and as wide as possible. The elite 20% is open to everyone who dreams a big enough dream and I hope to see you at the top very soon.

Recommended links:

- http://www.CraigBeck.com

- http://www.PowerfullyWealthy.com
- http://www.SubAttraction.com
- http://www.StopDrinkingExpert.com

THE MINDSET OF THE SUPER RICH

BUILDING EXTREME WEALTH

CRAIG BECK

The Millionaire Coaching Program

www.PowerfullyWealthy.com

Life is harsh right? But if you work long and hard you can ease the struggle… no pain, no gain!

Wrong, wrong, wrong! Virtually everything you have been told about how to have a happy, successful life is wrong. Not just a little bit wrong but the exact polar opposite of the truth!

So many people spend an entire lifetime not quite having enough… they get stuck in a job they don't like, in a relationship that isn't healthy and struggle along always with not quite enough money.

Life is not meant to be a struggle, money is not supposed to be scarce and you are not here to spend half your precious time on this planet working in a job that doesn't fulfill you and leaves you wondering what the point of it all is!

- *Yes I know you read 'The Secret' & it didn't work the way you hoped.*
- *Yes I know you tried positive thinking & found it impossible to maintain.*
- *Yes I know you have read self-help books & a hundred other things.*

Why didn't any of that work and why don't you have the life you dream of?

The truth has been sanitized to appeal to a mass market—remember, what I am about to show you flies in the face of what virtually everyone currently believes. Only a very select few people will be open-minded enough to be able to process this knowledge.

I do not advertise this website… Most people never find this coaching program; there is a reason you are here. You should trust me on this because a uniquely magical experience is just a mouse click away. Why not decide now and join my Manifesting Magic Coaching Program today?

I want you to be the next person whose life completely changes beyond their wildest dreams.

Part One

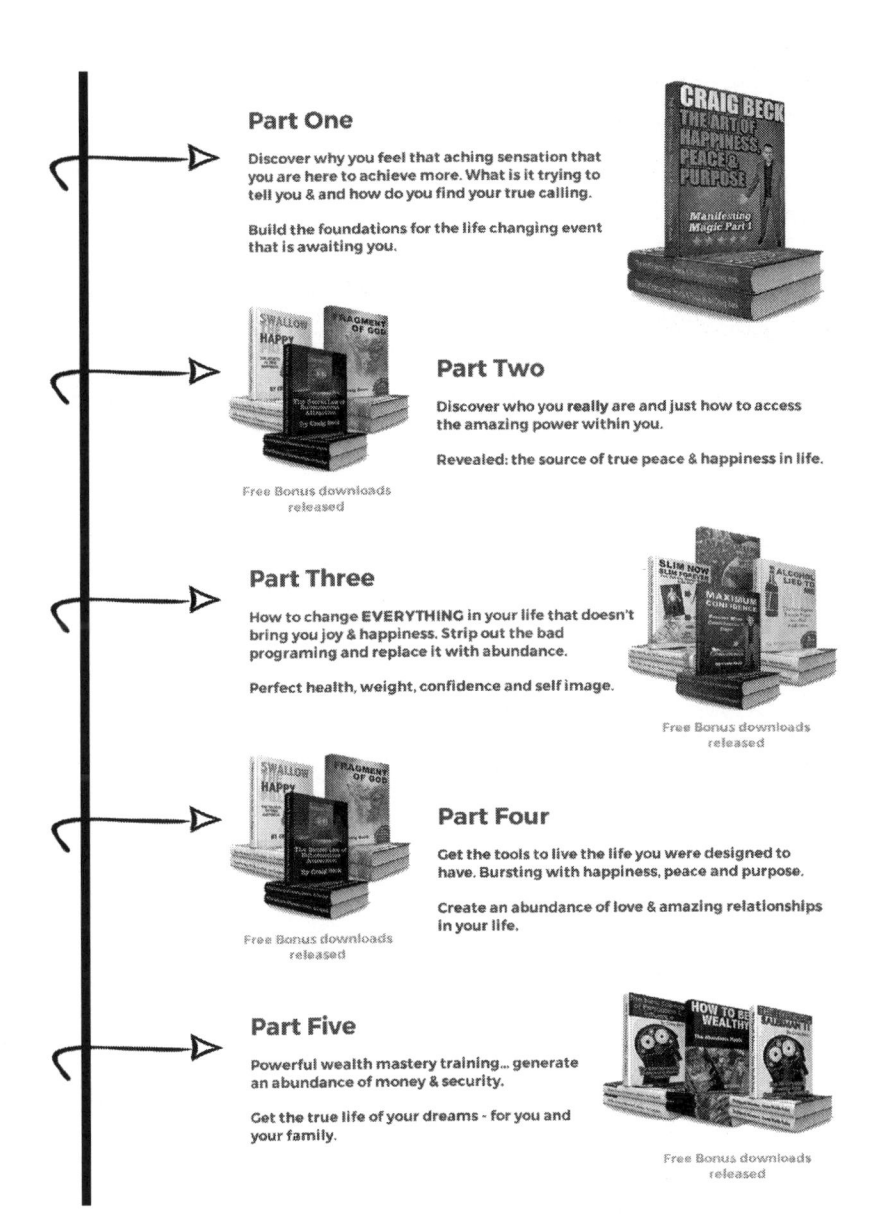

Discover why you feel that aching sensation that you are here to achieve more. What is it trying to tell you & and how do you find your true calling.

Build the foundations for the life changing event that is awaiting you.

Part Two

Discover who you **really** are and just how to access the amazing power within you.

Revealed: the source of true peace & happiness in life.

Free Bonus downloads released

Part Three

How to change **EVERYTHING** in your life that doesn't bring you joy & happiness. Strip out the bad programing and replace it with abundance.

Perfect health, weight, confidence and self image.

Free Bonus downloads released

Part Four

Get the tools to live the life you were designed to have. Bursting with happiness, peace and purpose.

Create an abundance of love & amazing relationships in your life.

Free Bonus downloads released

Part Five

Powerful wealth mastery training... generate an abundance of money & security.

Get the true life of your dreams - for you and your family.

Free Bonus downloads released

www.PowerfullyWealthy.com

Made in the USA
Middletown, DE
05 March 2018